The Art of Critical Making

Rhode Island School of Design on Creative Practice

Edited by Rosanne Somerson
and Mara L. Hermano
Foreword by John Maeda

Cover images: Elish Warlop (MFA 2013 Furniture Design), studies for
Rings of Fire and *Hoop Skirts* lighting, 2013, steel and brass, each 4 × 4 in.
Publication design: Julie Fry

This book is printed on acid-free paper. ∞

Published by John Wiley & Sons, Inc., Hoboken, New Jersey.
Published simultaneously in Canada.

For general information about our other products and services, please
contact our Customer Care Department within the United States
at (800) 762-2974, outside the United States at (317) 572-3993, or
fax (317) 572-4002.

Wiley publishes in a variety of print and electronic formats and by print-on-
demand. Some material included with standard print versions of this book
may not be included in e-books or in print-on-demand. If this book refers
to media such as a CD or DVD that is not included in the version you
purchased, you may download this material at http://booksupport.wiley.com.
For more information about Wiley products, visit www.wiley.com.

ISBN 978-1-118-51786-4 (cloth); ISBN 978-1-118-76395-7 (ebk);
ISBN 978-1-118-76403-9 (ebk)

Printed in the United States of America

10 9 8 7 6 5 4 3 2 1

Contents

5 **Foreword**   John Maeda

11 **Preface**   Frank R. Wilson

19 **The Art of Critical Making: An Introduction**
Rosanne Somerson

32 **Groundwork**   Leslie Hirst

52 **Text and Context: Outward in All Directions**
Daniel Cavicchi

74 **Conversation: Drawing**   Patricia C. Phillips

94 **Thingking**   John Dunnigan

116 **Object Lessons**   Sarah Ganz Blythe

138 **Conversation: Materials**   Kelly Dobson

164 **Graphic Design, Storytelling, and the Making of Meaning**
Lucinda Hitchcock

190 **The Nature Imperative**   Neal Overstrom

210 **Conversation: Critique**   Eva Sutton

230 **Acting into the Unknown**   Pradeep Sharma

245 **Afterword**   Mara L. Hermano

ACKNOWLEDGMENTS   251

CONTRIBUTORS   253

ILLUSTRATIONS   261

INDEX   265

Foreword

John Maeda

I spent a large part of the '90s getting a PhD at Tsukuba University Institute of Art and Design, a largely closed-off, pristine educational enclave of Japanese master makers and thinkers. There were no computers to speak of, and the web hadn't really happened yet. It was a happy time, unfettered by the e-mails and other e-disruptions that fill all of our days today. I often found myself in the library—intently learning about the history of design through old publications from Ulm (a kind of post-Bauhaus school) and of course the Bauhaus itself.

Conversely, I had spent the decade prior affixed to a computer, at MIT. The '80s was the time when the first "undo" action was invented. Imagine a world without undo; I remember after I began studying at Tsukuba, I was in an ink-drawing class where I noticed that whenever I made an error, my hand would reach for command-Z on an invisible keyboard in my mind. I had to "unlearn" being digital. In doing so, I learned to truly appreciate the advantages of being a student—to get the chance to unlearn what I knew, in order to learn anew. This wonderful educational experience inspired me to become a teacher myself. I returned to MIT as a junior professor at the Media Lab, where I could bring some of my art and design education to bear.

While I was cloistered in Japan, the computer really started to take off. It was fast. And it kept getting faster, cheaper, and better. Digital art and design were largely panned by the art and design establishment because of their "lack of the human hand." In retrospect, I can see that this was a normal reaction to a dehumanizing technology going mainstream—much the same as John Ruskin's and William Morris's proud questioning of the Industrial Revolution. What I could see upon my return from Japan, having been traditionally educated in Bauhaus-style thinking, was that there was opportunity in this new medium, which, like others before it, could help harness unbelievable amounts of expressive power and creative energy. I felt that the tool—in this case the computer—had to be mastered for it to do the biddings of the artist and designer's hand, head, and heart.

As an advocate in the late '90s for artists and designers writing their own computer programs, I often got a lot of flack. The prevailing sentiment was, "Why should artists learn to code when there are tools like Photoshop?" My goal was to simply follow what I learned from my materials-based education at Tsukuba—that we needed to treat the computer as a new kind of material, and to master it deeply. This interest led me to develop a variety of systems for teaching computer programming to artists and designers, culminating in the Design by Numbers system in 1999. My graduate students Ben Fry and Casey Reas then built an even better system called Processing, which has vastly eclipsed my own work—suitably and proudly so. Today there are thousands of artists and designers programming with Processing to advance their ideas computationally.

And so, after twelve years teaching at MIT, my post as the 16th President of Rhode Island School of Design has been a homecoming back to the world of rigorous art and design. This book is all about the kinds of things I learned at Tsukuba, and frankly way, way more. Having stood in the same ultra-hot studios of our Glass department where alumnus and teacher Dale Chihuly forged his first physical thoughts, which would come to define evanescence, and in the same drawing studio where alumnus Gus Van Sant came as a RISD freshman, later making major movies like *Good Will Hunting* and *Milk*, I know I stand on the hallowed grounds of a kind of creative education "dojo" unlike any other place on earth.

At RISD, the integrity of the work comes from a place of criticality *and* materiality. Why does it exist? What existed before? What has influenced it? How is it made? Can it be made? Can we will it to be made? I find that the process of making work at RISD involves a kind of questioning that rivals a grand jury combined with a six-sigma manufacturing audit. Every stone, speck of dirt, and atom of oxygen must be turned over and examined in the light of the day in its present, past, and future. It is this kind of intensity that makes our unique brand of "critical making" so relevant to this day and age. We are all hungry for authenticity—the studied touch of a human hand, the thoughtfulness of a brilliant human mind, and a heart replenished with the warmth of another human heart.

In this digital age, there is a renewed curiosity about humanity, materiality, and all things physical, simply because much of the world has lost sight of them. You see little bits of this in the incongruity of putting faux wood-grain digital veneers on software apps. We are still in the very early days of art, design, and the computer—we have yet to have that "aha" moment when the physical world and the virtual world truly click together. For now, I see tremendous opportunity in studying and understanding traditional media—for in these materials is the root of all that we know and can truly believe.

At the same time, I know that a deeper understanding of computer code and computer-aided design and fabrication is also important. At RISD we have those efforts underway, led by Provost Rosanne Somerson and her advanced critical making initiatives. I'm not surprised by the number of corporations that have begun to knock on our door to ask for what a business or technology school can no longer do for them—which is to help them envision the future by engaging with some of the most creative thinkers and makers of our times.

After a life spent traversing the fields of technology, art, and design, my foremost conclusion is that there is great power in both fields taken separately, and in both fields put together. Reading this book, you will see why RISD is a symbol for art, design, and creativity the world over, and as such, can play a role as their advocate on national and international stages. That is why we have taken a leadership role in the movement to turn STEM (Science, Technology, Engineering, and Math) into STEAM in the United States by adding the "Arts," broadly defined. STEAM advocates for the federal government to integrate art and design with its growing emphasis on STEM education and research. By doing so, we will develop the creativity needed to drive our innovation economy forward and keep America competitive throughout this century. The critical making we teach here at RISD is what enables designers and artists to create objects, devices, and services that are more engaging, more efficient, and more human.

So, STEAM is embodied naturally at RISD. Nowhere is this more evident than at the 75-year-old Edna Lawrence Nature Lab. Filled with more than 80,000 samples of animal, plant, and mineral materials, it's a beautiful repository of everything from a taxidermied turkey to Brazilian butterflies to human bones. At RISD we teach students to understand humanity and nature from the core essence and architecture of life—by observing it and reproducing it on paper or in clay. Science is taught the way it was taught centuries ago, when artists and scientists were often the same person.

We have all seen that in the battle over education funding, the arts have been cut to make way for STEM education in public schools. As a lifelong STEM student, I know the possibilities inherent to those disciplines, but I also know that the way they are taught doesn't always lead to creative thinking, nor do they enable vitality and humanity to shine through. STEAM got on the federal government's radar when Rhode Island Congressman James Langevin introduced a House Resolution in 2011 in support of STEAM research and education. Around the same time, a Conference Board study was released, which said that nearly all employers view creativity as increasing in importance in the workplace, yet 85 percent say they can't find the creative applicants they seek. Leaders in both business and policy circles have begun to recognize the criticality of integrating the arts and design with the STEM fields.

Since then, pardon the expression, the movement picked up steam and has found its place on Sesame Street, at South by Southwest, and on the agendas of the National Science Foundation and the National Endowment for the Arts. Please visit http://stemtosteam.org to learn more about how you can be a part of this important effort to reveal the importance of art and design. I am proud to lead an institution that knows that art isn't just a "nice to have," but a "need to have."

I believe that art and design have critical roles to play in innovation in this next century, much like science and technology did in the last. The very methods revealed in this book will drive the new ideas, movements, and solutions to help us tackle the complex problems of our day. RISD students understand this: 71 percent of students surveyed from the RISD Class of 2011 responded that they are or want to be entrepreneurs; they are pioneering a new kind of "artrepreneurship" for our country.

It's heartening to watch our students and graduates rise to this challenge and to witness the ever-growing stream of visitors on campus who recognize that artists and designers will be the next change agents. We have greatly broadened the kind of employers that come to RISD now from our home base of creative industries to include technology companies, financial services, healthcare solutions providers, and even venture capital firms looking for artists and designers to propel new ideas. In 2012, we launched the inaugural class of Maharam STEAM Fellows in Applied Art and Design, which funds RISD students to pursue internships in the public and nonprofit sectors. Michael Maharam, the company's CEO, himself a visionary in the broader cultural implications of design, expressed it well when he said, "Maharam believes that creativity demonstrated through the arts and design will play an increasingly critical role in America's ongoing efforts to remain a dominant global force through both culture and commerce."

So much of RISD's inspiration and humanity fill these pages—but words pale in comparison to what we experience every day on our campus. So in closing, I invite you to take a train, car, or plane to visit us here in Providence, Rhode Island. If you are a lifelong creative person—knowing that you are if you've read this far—you will feel like you are truly at home. It's my honor to get to see that satisfaction every day in our students' faces, here at RISD.

Preface

Frank R. Wilson

All humans are born biologically gifted learners—recipients of a host of inheritances from ancestors we will never meet. This claim is not one of those plastic verbal posies tossed lightly from a Preface writer to inspiration-hungry readers. It is a straightforward fact about the strength of every person's connection to genetic heritage, and the reason for our astonishing capacity to acquire skill, knowledge, and understanding through physical experience, fulfilling the deepest instinctive intentions of the human mind itself. No matter who our forebears were or where they lived as individuals, as a group they learned to see beneath surfaces, to read meaning into the unfamiliar, and to adapt and survive not simply as a species, but as living individuals, in a future than could not be foreseen. But how did they do it?

The sources of our readiness are unimaginably remote, as the roots of human physical skill and intelligence extend into the past by millions of years. It seems likely that widespread climate and vegetation changes in Africa at the end of the Miocene epoch, more than 5 million years ago, increasingly forced tree-dwelling apes there to take their chances as bipedal ground dwellers. When this happened, the hand and the brain that we inherit were not what they are today. Much of what we know about the evolution of the human wrist and hand we owe to Lucy, who lived in the Afar region of Ethiopia 3¼ million years ago.[1] A chimpanzee-size ape whose existence became known because her fossilized skeletal remains were discovered by anthropologist Donald Johanson in November 1974, Lucy the matriarch together with the species named after her, *Australopithecus afarensis*, stand very near the dawn of human evolution.[2]

As chimp-like as she may have looked, Lucy was structurally very unlike the chimp in ways that offer major clues to the early stages of human evolution. The most obvious structural difference was in the design of her pelvis and the bones of her lower extremities, which marked her as a habitual upright walker, or bipedal. Not quite so obvious at first were the un-apelike anatomic features of her hand. An increase in the length of the thumb compared to the fingers and the ability to rotate the index and middle fingers on their long axis gave her the biomechanics needed for a variety of new grips and hand movements. For example, the "3-jaw chuck" is a grip that permits an irregularly shaped object (such as a stone) to be held securely between the thumb, index, and middle fingers. This grip is identical to that used by a baseball pitcher for an overarm pitch, and would have been extremely useful if the skill of throwing could be mastered for purposes of hunting or defense.

Lucy's longer thumb retained the muscle and tendon features of the ape hand, allowing enhanced independence of thumb movement. The addition of new rotational movements of the index and middle finger that were absent in the ape hand show Lucy's hand to have put her descendants—our ancestors—solidly on the path toward the functionally far more versatile grasping and handling organ that became the modern human hand. Subsequent structural changes, mainly on the side of the hand opposite the thumb, allowed improved finger-to-finger contact and a greatly expanded range of grips and movements—in effect, the biomechanical platform that paved the way for us to become adept and highly skilled users of an open-ended set of objects and tools.

The hand of tree-living apes who lived millions of years before Lucy was itself highly specialized, but mainly for supporting and transporting the weight of the suspended body, for grooming and fighting, and for handling food and small objects available in the environment. Over time, minor anatomic changes produced a hand whose functions were being radically transformed; it was a hand that traded some of the raw power of the ape hand for a movement profile emphasizing independence of the thumb and greatly increased control of precision finger movements. The other major change (the oblique squeeze grip, which came after Lucy's time) compensated for power loss by increasing the effective power and accuracy that could be delivered by objects securely held and precisely controlled in the hand.

No one knows how much aggressive or defensive overarm throwing the *Australopithecines* actually did, nor do we know exactly when subsequent changes in the anatomy of the hand occurred or how they may have been exploited by Lucy's descendants, but we do know that over the span of several million years, those of Lucy's descendants who learned to take advantage of the hand came to dominate the bipedal world of the hominids and eventually outlasted all their competitors. When our ancestors came down from the trees, in other words, an upright walking posture had not merely relieved the forelimbs of their primary role in locomotion but had opened the door to a completely novel domain of perception, action, and *interaction* based in the hands. It was *our* ancestors who walked through that door.

The extremely long span of time from the earliest manufacture of stone tools until more complex objects appeared at habitation sites has been puzzling to some experts, but during that time there may have been little need for a more advanced tool "technology," and a significant portion of that time may have passed as the brain was altering its own operations to allow more complex movements of the hand and arm to be added to the already impressive repertoire of skilled upper limb movements that existed in chimpanzees. This is because the brain would not have been capable of controlling the complex movements of the evolving hominid hand *before* the hand itself was physically capable of varying the hand grips and individual finger movements which are now part of our repertoire.

Neural adaptation to a hand whose inner mechanics were in transition must have been extremely complicated for two other reasons: first, significant changes in hand function would have required an open-ended repertoire of adaptive body movements to make hand use effective and dependable—think of a carpenter hammering on a roof, a tennis player running toward the net, a short-order cook juggling pots and skillets on a stove. Second, as pointed out by anthropologist Peter C. Reynolds, human tool use eventually acquired a critical social dimension. As he says: "The essence of human technical activity is anticipation of the action of the other person and the performance of an action complementary to it, such that the two people together produce physical results that could not be produced by the two actions done in series by one person."[3]

There will always be room for debate about critical events in early human evolution, but it is widely conjectured by anthropologists, archeologists, and cognitive scientists alike that the biologic success of humans has largely been due to evolving hands, an increasing reliance on tools, and a host of behavioral changes associated with a complex communal and material culture. Given all of this, from a neurologic and evolutionary perspective, the conservative position on hand-brain co-evolution must be that the brain developed its enormously enhanced hand control capabilities very gradually and modified them over time as experience defined the long-term role of the hand in hominid survival. Genetic change at the species level assured that each new member of our species would arrive with an inborn potential for skilled hand use, activated by an early-life urge to take things apart and put them back together again, and to gain membership in a team in the process.

So what does Lucy's story have to do with the hands-on critical making at the core of art and design education at RISD? To answer that we must consider the current educational alternative. We live in an age of remarkable technological advances. Yet with all the good technology has done to add to the general prosperity of society, the as-yet-unmeasured cost of our acceptance of these advances in educational settings seems fundamentally at odds with the physicality of human perception, thought, and action. Computer and communications technologies have arrived in classrooms at every level, but the spectacular advances in student achievement widely anticipated from the digital revolution simply have not been realized.[4] As a society we have not learned how to use powerful new technologies in ways that do not paradoxically subvert the innate power of students to examine and learn that will lead them toward mastery on their own terms. The danger is that today's students, equipped with technologies they did not themselves create and which yield them experiences they are not prepared for or temptations they cannot resist, are at the mercy of the inevitably self-assertive tendencies of technologies.[5] Considering our hopes for them, and the inestimable power of resources already provided them by virtue of biological heritage, this seems not merely a tragic but an entirely needless outcome.

There is no such thing as just saying no to technology—there really never was. Lucy and the *Australopithecines* were a species on a very specific path, with a new arm, a new hand, and a brain capable of turning simple stones into a powerful hunting and self-defense technology. But Lucy also put her descendants on a path toward a unique kind of individual intelligence: a marriage of brain, body, and objects waiting to be turned into something better than what was already there. And that was not all: Objects brought to life by a maker return the favor, not only by fostering confidence and vitality but by sharpening personal identity and adding meaning to the experience of consciousness.

That for humans there should be an essential reciprocity between action and identity, mediated by the hand, is neither modern nor merely an interesting idea—it is a signature motif found over and over in the work of late Renaissance artists, elevated to the status of religious iconography in Michelangelo's *The Creation of Adam*. My own relation to this idea grew over many years working as a neurologist with musicians at virtually all stages of their education and their careers, an experience that led me to believe that the desire to achieve an artistic goal is invariably strengthened when the body itself is both the instrument and the focus of the work. There must be many reasons why this is so, but one that should stand out for readers of this book is that when physical skill supports and enlivens the creative process, memories of place, object, movement, and companions will always make their way into the fabric of achievements.

We are now well into the computer revolution and the information age, living with changes in virtually every aspect of ordinary and professional life. The way bankers handle money, armies fight wars, writers get their books published, politicians get elected—everything has changed. Well, almost everything: gymnasts still balance on narrow beams and risk injury from falling; violinists still perform on violins whose design has been stable for centuries; cowboys still ride real horses; hairdressers still use scissors to cut hair; potters still throw pots on a rotating wheel. What about architects and engineers? What about designers and doctors? What about you and me? No matter what computers do for us, gaining mastery of the body and deploying it as an agent of the mind may be the only way for us as individuals to continue to find the distinctive and emotionally rich forms of creative expression that embodied learning makes possible, and to retain control of the idiosyncratic, mysterious self that came along with the rest of the package.

Notes

1. We also owe a great deal to anthropologist Mary Marzke at Arizona State University, whose contributions to our understanding of the evolution of modern hand function are grounded in her landmark research on Lucy and on the evolution of hand and wrist morphology in relation to hand use and the manufacture of stone tools. See Mary Marzke, "Who Made Stone Tools?" in *Stone Knapping: The Necessary Conditions for a Uniquely Hominid Behavior*, McDonald Institute Monographs, Valentine Roux and Blandine Bril, eds. (Cambridge, UK: Oxbow Books, 2005).

2. The discovery of Lucy and the aftermath of the find are described in Donald Johanson and Maitland Edey's *Lucy: The Beginnings of Humankind* (New York: Simon & Schuster, 1981).

3. Peter C. Reynolds, "The Complementation Theory of Language and Tool Use," in *Tools, Language, and Cognition in Human Evolution*, Kathleen R. Gibson and Tim Ingold, eds. (Cambridge, UK: Cambridge University Press, 1993), 412.

4. It has probably been a full decade since one could have anything approaching a clear idea about the direction and influence of computers and the media on education. The years surrounding the millennium were a time of lively and confident writing on the subject: Stephen Talbott's *The Future Does Not Compute: Transcending the Machines in Our Midst* (Sebastopol, CA: O'Reilly & Associates, Inc., 1995); Jane M. Healy's *Failure*

to Connect: How Computers Affect Our Children's Minds—for Better and Worse (New York: Simon & Schuster, 1998); Alison Armstrong and Charles Casement, *The Child and the Machine: Why Computers May Put Our Children's Education at Risk* (Toronto: Key Porter Books, 1998); C. A. Bowers, *Let Them Eat Data: How Computers Affect Education, Cultural Diversity, and the Prospects for Ecological Sustainability* (Athens, GA: University of Georgia Press, 2000). 2000 was also the year *U.S. News and World Report* featured a young girl on its cover, seated rather improbably on a lawn, intently gazing at the screen of a portable computer, next to the title "Why Computers Fail as Teachers: Too Much Screen Time Can Harm Your Child's Development" (September 25, 2000). Probably the last serious book in this genre was Todd Oppenheimer's *The Flickering Mind: The False Promise of Technology in the Classroom and How Learning Can Be Saved* (New York: Random House, 2003). A decade later you know who won the epic battle from today's book titles. From Sherry Turkle, MIT's Professor of the Social Studies of Science and Technology, we have a blunt description of our new way of living: *Alone Together: Why We Expect More from Technology and Less from Each Other* (New York: Basic Books, 2011); and from Kevin Kelly, co-founder and Executive Editor of *Wired* magazine, we have our marching orders: *What Technology Wants* (New York: Penguin Books, 2010). There is a consolation prize, though. Our individual minds may have become a shadow of what our parents had (or vainly thought they had), but they are connected! For a vision of how education will look when the shouting is finally over, see: *Connected Learning: An Agenda for Research and Design, a Research Synthesis of the Connected Learning Research Network* (Irvine, CA: The MacArthur Foundation on Digital Media and Learning Research Hub, January 2013).

5. For an excellent discussion on this topic, see Catherine Dowling's recent paper, "The Hand: Kinesthetic Creation and the Contemporary Classroom," *The International Journal of Learning* 8, no. 18 (2012): 51–66. See also Matthew B. Crawford, *Shop Class as Soulcraft: An Inquiry into the Value of Work* (New York: The Penguin Press, 2009), especially Chapter 6, "The Contradictions of the Cubicle"; and Richard Sennett, *The Craftsman* (New Haven, CT: Yale University Press, 2009), especially "Fractured Skills: Hand and Head Divided."

The Art of Critical Making: An Introduction

Rosanne Somerson

Walk along the riverfront in Providence, Rhode Island, at the foot of "College Hill," and you may be surprised by what you see. You might easily walk beside someone carrying a hollow six-foot shoe fabricated from woven wire, or alongside a group of students balancing their newly finished chairs on their backs and heads, or pass someone lugging a drawing portfolio so large and unwieldy that you might be tempted to stop and ask to assist. On certain days there could be fashion collections wheeled on hanger racks, or recycled industrial off-cuts of felt and cork spilling out of bags slung over shoulders, or even sculpted metal chopsticks three times the height of the woman hauling them. Someone might have laced delicate woven yarn around trees lining the river walk, preparing their branches with sweater-like covers for winter. Out of sight, inside the studios and labs, a diverse range of projects could likely be developing—investigations into sustainable systems for food transport, or objects designed for extreme climates, or a video that correlates and weaves together two events happening simultaneously in different locations.

Art schools are lively places, but few outside their walls have the opportunity to experience the kind of environment where the new is manifest every day, where paradigms are continually stretched and challenged, and where shock and beauty flourish side by side. What is the "magic" in the art and design school learning model that advances an individual from an interested student into a creative innovator? And how might the creativity and expertise that result from this form of education be accessible to others? While no single philosophy or pedagogy effectively turns developing artists and designers into creative professionals, some shared methods have proven to transform hard-working students into exceptional creative practitioners. In this book, RISD faculty and staff examine these methods to explore RISD's rationale and approach in developing and enhancing creative learning. Additionally, we explore the efficacy and the *essential need*, in contemporary times, for learning that includes hands-on practice, the processing of enhanced seeing and perception, and contextualized understanding—all elements of "critical making."

At RISD we develop curricular models through which innovation and originality are coaxed, rendered, and challenged, leading to heightened expression and new ways of thinking. We cultivate intense personal development, deep disciplinary expertise, rigorous skill-building, advanced conceptual reasoning, and attention to both process and execution. We are committed to fostering creative and critical thinkers who innovate with ease, who are not rattled by uncertainty, who move agilely from one form of output to another, and who can communicate in multiple ways with acuity and clarity. We believe that these traits are effective remedies for crumbling systems and structures that no longer work. As educational systems propel us further and further away from physical, tangible experience, how better might learning support nimble, innovative, and imaginative thinking than through models that emphasize the iterative formation of ideas through making? Contemporary times call for contemporary thinkers and makers.

Through these pages, we invite you to enter with us into a world of creative energy and rigorous investigation. Who might benefit from a "peek through the keyhole" into the multifaceted characteristics of RISD's educational practice? This book will certainly be useful to those who are directly pursuing an art and design education. Prospective students will gather deep insights into their potential futures. Parents who may be skeptical about the benefits of supporting such a path at a time when it seems that key opportunities point toward other areas of study—business, technology, scientific research, entertainment, medicine, and marketing—may be surprised to learn that RISD alumni have succeeded at high levels in remarkable ways in all of these fields. A RISD alumna who later became an attorney still cites her RISD education as the formative basis for complex problem solving required in her law practice; a product designer demonstrates that his education in design process helped him to create one of the most successful online businesses in existence; some of the region's best restaurants famous for their remarkably innovative cuisine boast RISD alumni as chefs and owners. Our alumni are successful recording artists, medical device inventors, and social visionaries who have changed and improved lives around the world. And of course the list of distinguished alumni artists and designers representing every form of creative practice is the source of great pride. RISD graduates have made Oscar-winning films (and even hosted the Oscars), popular book and television series, and significant public programming. The number of alumni who have been awarded MacArthur "genius" Fellowships and Fulbrights is unmatched by any other art school. Look at the "Gallery Guide" in any city, attend any global art fair, or visit any of the top design, architecture, fashion, or textile firms, and you will likely find numerous RISD alumni at work. In short, extraordinary results have emerged from the RISD educational experience as it has evolved over some 135 years.

In addition to aspiring young artists and designers and their parents, many others will find this book enlightening and supportive. Many corporations recognize how much more inventive they can be when they apply principles like those framed in our curricula, paying close attention to how they activate innovation and advance opportunity. Businesses of all sorts looking for ways to rethink long-held assumptions and to build greater creativity into their process and outcomes will find illuminating and expansive approaches to familiar questions, which may well generate innovation and new achievement. Practitioners early in their careers looking for ways to build their own strong creative practices will benefit from the insights of the experienced educators who have contributed to this book, gaining deeper understanding of high-level creative learning. Even other systems of education can benefit from echoing the curricular approaches and processes of an art and design institution such as RISD. Indeed, so much about art and design education can benefit a broad audience.

The writers who have contributed to this book—like all of our faculty, staff, and librarians—lead in their disciplines through engaged and ongoing professional practice. These writers do not attempt here to define art or design.

They do not offer a prescription for creative innovation. Instead, they offer observations and examples from direct experience that make up the substance and distinction of a RISD education, untangling the territory of art education, which remains largely unknown outside of arts institutions. Through our contributors' careful telling, RISD's remarkably effective methodologies and tools for transformative education can be accessed by any curious reader.

In the Preface, neurologist, author, and researcher Frank Wilson—the only writer in this book who is not a faculty or staff member at RISD (though he is a frequent RISD visitor and lecturer)—describes the biologic science of the co-evolution of the hand and the brain, and proposes the resulting neurological precedents to thinking and making as collaborators in both human and educational development. He sets the stage for the other contributors, who echo how the artistic mind relies on "making" as a critical activity, one that informs a particular kind of deep intelligence that cannot be learned without real material manipulation and sensory, embodied experience.

Leslie Hirst, Foundation Studies faculty member, presents the "groundwork" of preparing students to become immersive learners in our common undergraduate first year, literally laying the foundation for the commitment it takes to succeed as a creative professional. The first-year experience for freshmen, and, in different ways, for graduate students, is about learning how to reset expectations, to find new ways to begin, and to develop the conceptual and making tools necessary to create works that are significant in composition, presentation, function, or solution. The first year is about devising individual systems for making and breaking one's own rules. As Hirst notes, it is also about learning to live comfortably in uncertainty so as to take new risks and forge new directions, and to push harder through personal limitations than ever imagined. These fundamental and formative experiences contribute to building the experience and bodies of knowledge that shape an artist or designer.

The creative process cannot live independently from the contexts that inform the maker. In his essay, Dean of Liberal Arts Daniel Cavicchi describes how the rigorous Liberal Arts courses required of every RISD student deepen scholarship, research practices, and forms of expression. Inquiry takes many forms in an art and design environment, and at RISD we believe that multiple research methodologies are paramount to developing innovative thinking and making and to educating informed future citizens—a goal at the heart of RISD's mission. RISD students draw connections to histories, philosophies, literary forms, and identities—all essential to building ethical, reflective, self-aware, and articulate practices. Cavicchi describes how RISD students thus "develop a familiarity with meta-thinking which, in turn, heightens their ability to see new connections and meanings." Liberal Arts courses create context that informs studio work, just as art and design students bring into their Liberal Arts classrooms unique and imaginative forms of inquiry.

Three topics in this book—drawing, materials, and critique—are so essential to a RISD education, and yet so diversely implemented, that we chose to present them as guided "Conversations," incorporating numerous voices to express multiple approaches. The first "Conversation," led by Dean of Graduate Studies Patricia Phillips, explores drawing. Drawing is fundamental to RISD learning. Drawing helps to develop the intelligence of the hand and its cooperation with the eye and the brain. Drawings are a required component of our undergraduate admissions application, and help to determine who gets accepted into RISD. We use these application drawings, however, not just to evaluate who "draws well" but to help us assess how an applicant *sees*.

To non-artists, drawing is often understood as replicating or representing what is seen—capturing shape and contour, composition, outlines, and shadows in space. At RISD, though mastering various representation techniques may be part of skill-building, drawing is regarded more as what Phillips calls a "flexible instrument," a developmental tool, a way of mapping thinking that can be circuitous, improvisational, or highly structured. Drawing also helps us to record events and ideas and share them with someone else. It can be a container for curiosity, banking undeveloped ideas to percolate into something later. I still refer to sketchbooks that I made as a sophomore, many years ago. The "raw" ideas in those pages engender completely new resonance to me today, and in some instances have manifested as projects decades later.

When we turn drawings into things, how do those things emulate or express the thinking that helped to bring them to life? In "Thingking," Professor John Dunnigan merges thinking and making into one action word, highlighting their symbiotic relationship. Dunnigan proposes that embodied knowledge is a direct result of engaging with real materials and real scale. He articulates a clear philosophy about how both research and conceptual development emerge in physical form, exemplifying curricular outcomes in the work of alumni.

One special place where RISD students and the public encounter extraordinary examples of real-scale objects is in the RISD Museum. RISD is fortunate to have as part of the college a world-class art museum, which contains more than 80,000 objects originating from classical times to the present and representing most regions of the world. These great works serve as fertile sources of knowledge. They help us to understand fabrication methods across millennia, as well as broad aspects of culture ranging from aesthetics to social structures to spirituality. Sarah Ganz Blythe, Director of Education at the RISD Museum, describes the long history of learning from objects as primary sources by looking, analyzing, and contextualizing. Such learning helps us form a language for communicating responses to art and design, and in turn fosters the creation of art and design objects that speak their own language. Suggesting that works of art rarely have finite or singular meanings, Ganz Blythe demonstrates that interpretation is a form of expression open to not only artists and designers but to all museum visitors.

The Museum is a wonderful laboratory in which to look at not just works of art but the materials they are made of, and how those have both changed and remained consistent over time. We are fortunate that our Fleet Library now includes the Graham Visual + Material Resource Center, an amazing, growing collection of tens of thousands of materials for exploration and research—some commercial materials, some natural materials, and some materials that students have created themselves. Materials have played an essential role in the development of works of art and design throughout time. Indeed, early historic periods were named and designated by materials—the Stone Age, the Iron Age, and so on. Today, material studies are complex and multiply scaled—from molecular investigations to research on the environmental impacts of procurement and distribution. The materials collection provides a platform through which to address these issues, with a particular focus on principles of sustainability.

Materials are deep at the heart of making at RISD, playing key and diverse roles. Their exploration comprises the second of our "Conversations," this one led by Associate Professor Kelly Dobson, Head of our Digital + Media graduate program. Dobson interviewed three RISD faculty members and the Visual + Material Resource Librarian. Each participant has varied and intimate experience with materials in his or her work and teaching. Dobson and her colleagues' perspectives challenge us to regard materials both pragmatically and conceptually, showing how material explorations and applications operate in both orthodox and innovative ways. The conversations address not just the application of materials, but how sensitized responses to materials can allow the material, rather than the maker, to lead. Materials can be virtual as well, which means that now, like never before, artists and designers have a wider palette with which to express their ideas.

Lucinda Hitchcock, Professor in Graphic Design, addresses another profound change in our times—the influx of information and the form that makes that information evident. Hitchcock describes how visual narrative, or storytelling, can provide paths to navigate, interpret, and frame the many ways in which we encounter and process unfiltered information. She has been part of a faculty team for many years at RISD that has evolved a signature course called "Making Meaning." Meaning is at the heart of communication, and through this course students develop visual forms of expression that facilitate understanding. Providing evocative descriptions of cultural phenomena and examples from the classroom and student work, Hitchcock helps us to understand how today's graphic designers are "cultural curators," producing the information that defines and enhances our experiences every day.

The natural world provides its own kind of meaning. Another of RISD's particular treasures is the Edna Lawrence Nature Lab, an inspiring collection of natural specimens ranging from plants, insects, and skeletons to rocks, shells, and amoebas to various forms of taxidermy animals and even a few live species. A fundamental part of a RISD education for 75 years, the Nature Lab is a center for examination and comparison and for learning from nature's systems. Students study how efficient systems can produce elegant results, and then apply that learning to other contexts. They explore consistencies and inconsistencies at various scales, from galaxies to microscopic worlds. The Nature Lab's Director, Neal Overstrom, a design-scientist with a background in both design and biology, is uniquely adept at guiding artists and designers to draw both information and inspiration from this magical collection. In his essay, "The Nature Imperative," Overstrom describes how the Lab helps students to develop sensitivity, observation, and perception, and why this kind of learning matters.

Throughout the developmental stages of creation, art and design education depends on critiques—or "crits" as they are commonly referred to at RISD—as a unique learning mode. At a crit, students present their work to reviewers, articulate their intentions, and receive feedback. The reviewers might be faculty, students and faculty, or a group that includes external professional reviewers. Often these external critics are from other disciplines, bringing a fresh perspective to the work.

Critiques are core to the development and assessment of creative work. Highly diverse in their methods and outcomes, they adhere to no single formula. In this book's third "Conversation," Professor Eva Sutton asked several faculty, students, and alumni to each make a sketch representative of his or her experience of critique, then used the sketches as a basis for exploring the various modes of critique. Critiques can be behavioral learning experiences that help participants learn about social interaction, expressions of support, and disagreement. Successful critiques are about perceptive, constructive feedback, not a judgment of good or bad, but an offering of "I experience this—was that your intention?" or "What if…?" Critiques provide a pathway through which students develop a lifelong ability to self-evaluate and to reflect on improving, articulating, and evolving their ideas. The benefits of this kind of conscious awareness of how a work succeeds in communicating an intended outcome and the cultivation of honest response surely have applications not just in art and design but in multiple circumstances.

In "Acting into the Unknown," Dean of Architecture and Design Pradeep Sharma describes how we take art and design learning out into the world—how various forms of creativity and innovation can influence creative practices of all sorts as well as business models, and ultimately mark culture itself. Sharma describes the various structures of our partnered engagements, from short executive-education salons to long-term partnered research projects that we have run with a range of corporations, industries, and government agencies such as NASA. Partners collaborate with RISD to explore issues using our creative methodologies—to frame new questions and advance opportunities. Our iterative process leads to new directions for exploration, and our ability to manifest ideas in real form through making materializes ideas. As Sharma suggests, this is often where true innovation occurs.

The gifted contributors to this book each articulate an important aspect of a potent, adventurous form of teaching and learning. While this book celebrates the excellence of a RISD education, it is also about showcasing the value of an art and design education in principle, using RISD as a model. Recently there has been a surge of interest in the particular character of art and design education and how its ingredients build both the intuitive and rational abilities that generate change. Studies and the media are full of examples of creative approaches applied in new contexts, as business schools incorporate "design thinking" into curricula, businesses apply creative processes to planning and decision-making, and companies hire CIOs (Chief Innovation Officers). A plethora of books about creativity, problem solving, and innovation has been published in the past few years. RISD's President, John Maeda, has worked with government representatives such as Rhode Island Representative Jim Langevin and numerous bi-partisan Congressional representatives to add art and design to the national Science, Technology, Engineering, and Math (STEM) education agenda, incorporating an "A" for "art and design" to turn STEM into STEAM. This platform, supported now in over 30 countries around the globe, recognizes art and design as the "secret sauce" in multiple fields, engaging with creative exploration to reach greater potential—the potential that will help to define advancements in the twenty-first century.

Being Provost of RISD at such a significant time in history is intensely rewarding. As the world grows increasingly complex and fast-paced, with global issues impacting us all, making, materials, and meaning are critical. The kind of essential knowing that we develop at RISD—informed through our hands, through our bodies, and in the creation of works, experiences, and events—is more cogent than at any other time. Artists and designers hone the capacity to generate something from deep inside ourselves to live *outside* of ourselves. By residing in the experiential and the physical, and by developing the "hands-on" as a portal of intelligent learning, we confirm the mind as maker and making as a state of mindfulness. We demonstrate how artists and designers are hosts for enduring creative discovery that is self-initiated and actively engaged. In short, artists and designers manifest what has not existed previously—in many cases, what has never even been imagined.

A group of 34 forward-thinking women—members of the Rhode Island Centennial Committee—envisioned the importance of art and design as the key to progress and to humanizing and enhancing culture when they founded

RISD in 1877. Their early mission was three-fold. First, to teach "artisans in drawing, painting, modeling, and designing, that they may successfully apply the principles of Art to the requirements of trade and manufacture." Second, they wanted to train "students in the practice of Art, in order that they may understand its principles, give instruction to others, or become artists." Third, they intended to advance "public Art Education, by the exhibition of works of Art and of Art school studies, and by lectures on Art." RISD's current mission reflects all of these goals, with an expanded emphasis on discovering and transmitting knowledge to make "lasting contributions to a global society through critical thinking, scholarship, and innovation." This recent addition to the mission, while new in some ways, is very much in keeping with the notion of showcasing expertise and innovation through world's fairs. The form and forum may have changed, but not the intent.

Indeed, the intentions of an art and design education as envisioned in 1877 are still relevant today. RISD remains committed to immersive disciplinary learning as fundamental to evolving basic principles into new contexts. Still, as disciplinary boundaries conflate and overlap, we are emphasizing ways to encourage crossovers and new forms of research and practice. At RISD, as in broader contemporary culture, the familiar delineations between artist and designer are becoming less distinct; disciplinary boundaries are more like placeholders for definition rather than parameters. In the professional world, artists are creating successful design work and vice versa. RISD students are encouraged to integrate diverse practices in developing their work. Architecture students immerse themselves in fine arts courses and painters can learn the techniques and processes of designers. This kind of integrated learning complements disciplinary expertise, in which structured curricula call forth deep, immersive investigation, intensive trial and error, and critical feedback.

Today, new models emanating from art and design are helping us to live and work more flexibly, effectively, and meaningfully in a world that is rapidly changing and economically challenging. We need confident, creative, and nimble thinkers who can navigate circuitous complexity. The meandering

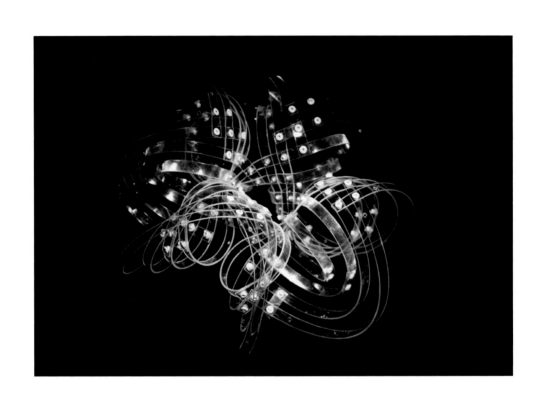

lines of Laura Kishimoto's (BFA 2013 Furniture Design) beautiful object, *Medusa*, symbolically illustrate this kind of agility, where transparent lines still achieve solid form, punctuated by highlights all along the way (fig. 1). Our economies, our cultural entities, and even our own constructed lives require generative contributions that, rather than seek a single answer or follow a mapped path, open many doors of possibility and often benefit from the surprises of serendipity. *The Art of Critical Making* showcases how an education in art and design contributes to just these models and approaches, exploring the core principles that guide this kind of journey, a journey that is not directional, but dimensional.

Fig. 1
Laura Kishimoto,
Medusa, 2013

Groundwork

Leslie Hirst

How does a new student of art and design transform into a creative and critical maker? Leslie Hirst, Associate Professor, Foundation Studies, argues that critical making is not something that just happens to people with certain gifts or abilities. Rather, critical making—transforming the ordinary into something meaningful—involves absolute focus and an enormous amount of doing that is often hard to qualify while it is being done. Through recollections and a series of lessons, Hirst demonstrates that the path to becoming a creative practitioner is never straight, and is strewn with obstacles as well as inspiration.

Throughout grade school I was accused of being "creative." For this reason, whenever our class was required to partake in a group art project, the teacher put me in charge. It is easy to recall the burden of this label. It meant that I was expected to pull something foreign or surprising out of myself even though I had always considered my ideas normal and obvious, and I didn't think I ever demonstrated that I was capable of anything else. I was certain at age seven or ten that others had misidentified my talents. I felt like a fraud. Simply, I was very good at making exactly what I wanted to make look exactly as it should look. It had not occurred to me that most people have no concept how this is done.

I grew up around makers, but not around artists. Perhaps necessity, limitations, and isolation fueled my need to "make" more than the desire to express or adorn. I watched my father soldering circuit boards that led to the booming bass from a stereo speaker, and my mother pour cake batter into two round pans that when baked, she cut, reconfigured, and frosted into a flop-eared bunny, and my grandmother carefully place crumbly bulbs into a plot of dirt that sprouted yellow and red tulips the next year. The transformation of materials by human hands captivated me, and these experiences likely enabled me to see something else when looking directly at any image, object, or event.

I bring up these accounts not only to place myself within a framework for discussing creativity, but also because they establish a ground for disseminating the elastic, ambiguous, unpredictable, and mysterious qualities that surround the term "creative." Too often, the word is carelessly attached to anything new or different. Just as frequently it is used to denote skill or fanciness even though no real innovation has taken place. Perhaps it is also an accessible word to identify something that (or someone who) is not easily understood. In any case, these casual inferences reflect a host of personal traits and qualities, from free-spirited to analytical, messy to precision-oriented, or just plain difficult to categorize, putting those who are labeled "creative" into a very varied group.

Psychologists and behavioral scientists agree that creativity is a complex combination of attributes, including but not restricted to knowledge, personality type, and environment, and that it manifests differently depending on one's motivation.[1] Likewise, the presence of creative tendencies is believed to be the result of both nature and nurture, as not all children of electricians, bakers, or gardeners will exhibit interest or aptitude in creative practices. It is curious, then, that without a firm definition of what it is, where it comes from, and how it can be measured, creative thinking is a respected human characteristic positioned high on the list of desired student outcomes for most educational institutions. After all, given these variables, it would seem that the ability to teach someone to think creatively is a failed proposition from the outset. Yet, every fall I enter a classroom full of wide-eyed, optimistic, and intelligent young students with that objective in mind.

For most of my academic career, I have taught multidisciplinary studio fundamentals, commonly known as Foundation Studies, to first-year college art and design students. I feel fortunate to be involved with this early stage of students' development as each year a fresh crop of individuals who were similarly deemed "creative types" enter my classes with some sort of vague idea about how their interests and abilities might be channeled to help them become makers of wonderful, important, transformative things. Eager and willing, they are each driven toward something that they can't quite define, with some sort of expectation for what their education will provide, and I want to make their discovery as accessible as it can be. But the bad news is that finding an authentic voice and direction in creative practices is hard and sloppy work, and each individual is responsible for making that discovery in her or his own way.

Helping students to arrive at this understanding is not easy, as the factors that play into developing a creative practice are as fluid and mutable as the definition of creativity itself. Whether we are practicing artists and designers or students wishing to enter these fields, our thinking is shaped by an accumulation of experiences and contacts from every aspect of life. On account of this, I have often said that I never teach the same course twice since the dynamic of the students' cultures, histories, and interests combine in drastically different ways with every new class roster. I imagine that this imperative subjectivity is not always the case for higher education courses, where, in certain disciplines anyway, a topic is taught and similar knowledge is gained in pretty much the same way by all of the students. In those scenarios, learning a subject is like filling a box with items numbered 1, 2, 3, 4, and 5 as certain achievements are met. However, in art and design education, what we gain is a box of question marks. These are not marks of misunderstanding; rather, they stand for possibilities. They don't ask the question "Why?" but instead ask "Why *not*?"

Inviting possibilities demands a great deal of trust in the uncertainty of the creative process, even though giving oneself over to uncertainty seems like an unlikely goal. I can draw upon my own, indirect journey to this understanding as a case in point. Indeed, creative impulses and sensibilities were part of my initial wiring, and I followed them into the fields of art and design. I came into academics much later, however, earning my bachelor's degree after a 16-year professional design career. It could be said that I approached my education backwards by learning the practice before learning the purpose of that practice. Having missed out on the aspects of learning that arise in a college setting, I felt the void of what had not been a part of my initial training—the immersive, cumulative, engendered knowledge, from the earliest records of thought until this day, and a constant influx of thinking permeating from all disciplines. These are essential components for bringing one's work to a level of excellence and they congeal when one embraces the wholeness of learning. Not all students understand why they are being taught certain things as some simply want to get to that place on the other side of graduation. But a student's job is to test assumptions, make mistakes, and question everything free from the confines of corporate or institutional protocol. Being a student demands humility and assurance that one's work can founder or collapse without an impact on the bottom line. These are the benefits of being a student that never happen in any of life's other forums, and they should be relished and exercised fully!

One of the first classes that I was hired to teach was a Foundation course entitled "Two-Dimensional Design." While I had been applying perceptive design skills and principles professionally for many years, in my own education I had been exempted from Foundation courses due to my experience and admissions portfolio, thus I had no models for teaching and learning in this area. I was perplexed to read in my supplied course outline that "color" was considered two-dimensional. This certainly didn't align with my experience, and seemed to be simply a convenient construct. So I referred to books in order to find out what teaching this topic would involve. Many of the sample exercises seemed formulaic and neutral, laying out abstract assignments that didn't reflect intellectual differences and interests. At the other extreme, examples were drawn from work by contemporary artists. Emulating either the conceptual or formal decisions of working artists will not teach one where the artists' decisions came from or how they were arrived at. These examples merely act as shortcuts to creative solutions, since the artists have already done the legwork.

To craft my own syllabus, I decided that presenting recipes was not a useful way to encourage students to think creatively and make critical decisions. Instead, I boiled everything down to the core of the ingredients, introducing the properties, histories, philosophies, language, technologies, and varieties of applications to re-sensitize the students' seeing and understanding, establish a platform for possibilities, and ask them to think and work in entirely new ways. In a manner, it is the classic mode of "breaking beginning students down in order to build them back up." This type of mental overhaul may sound extreme since young people today come into a world that is packed with visual information and process what they see in ways that we could not have imagined a quarter of a century ago. For a typical audience/viewer/user, this aptitude is adequate to navigate the saturated visual landscape. But makers need to exercise different types of mental processing. Our image-rich culture seduces the population with end products, and students today are drawn into areas of creative practice as they see themselves taking part in the lineage promised by the cool things that they see. Yet, making is not about the end—it is about the process.

In my teaching, I stress the importance of the creative process over the product, but the impact of how or when this shift in understanding takes place came into sharp focus only recently. In preparation for the final in my "Studio Design" course, I took my class to the Study Room at the RISD Museum to view a portfolio of paper folding structures by the artist Tauba Auerbach. The complex structural and color interactions in the portfolio make it a favorite to show to prospective students and parents who tour the collection, and it always garners "oohs and ahs" on those preliminary visits. I thought that seeing it might likewise inspire my students, but just 11 weeks into their first semester, they had a profoundly different reaction. As the portfolio opened, instead of witnessing surprised joy, I watched a roomful of heads and shoulders slump in desperation. I was startled to realize that little more than halfway through their first semester, my students were projecting themselves into this portfolio not with the passive eyes of spectators, but with the knowledge of makers. No longer just an end product to them, this portfolio now embodied hours of toil and experimentation, trial and error, measuring and calculating. Seeing it demonstrated to the students that if they wished to make successful work they needed to build up their creative muscles.

Truly, artists and designers are laborers, and the earlier we learn to roll up our sleeves and get to work, the better. "Possibilities" are tests of endurance, and one must be willing to do something over and over again until it is right or until something else is discovered. But how will we know what "right" is or what discovery looks and feels like? To begin, two main constants must be addressed: one involves identifying and observing underlying rules; the other involves breaking them.

Art and design are rule-based. This flies in the face of everything that most people have been taught before, namely, that art and design are about freedom. I remember reading a wonderful analogy about this concept many years ago in an out-of-print, early twentieth-century book on design.[2] The author asked us to imagine flying a kite—the quintessential emblem of unrestricted spontaneity, soaring in the wind. Keeping taut the line between you and the kite, however, is the source of that freedom. Here's another way of putting it: "Creativity arises out of the tension between the rules and imagination."[3]

Setting up a step-by-step framework of procedures is a good initiative toward promoting innovative problem solving, but those are not the kind of rules that I am talking about here. Structured guidelines can easily become comfortable formulas that inhibit noticing unanticipated directives. Imagine a person making an adventurous trek with a tour group versus a native explorer. When following a guide, the routes, stopovers, resources, and timetables have been determined, although each person still experiences a different set of sensations and forms unique responses. The native explorer, on the other hand, has learned to analyze subtleties in the weather, plan for resources, calculate distance, and ponder a host of other nuances that will prompt adjustments to the expedition's course. Needless to say, one route is predictable; the other is not.

The rule-based art and design that I am addressing is built upon standards of relevancy and application. By relevancy, I mean the ability to make judgments about one's own work in comparison to other aspects in life, which is a vital move toward self-criticality and creative thinking. Coming out of high school art programs, students often confuse creativity with originality, and they strive to do something that has not been done before with only a small window into what "before" is. Frequently, they have been directed to engage in personal expression that reflects their feelings and impulses, but have not developed the ability to discriminate between aesthetic concerns that are historical, biological, culturally specific, or merely style and fashion. Few of them have ever heard the word "kitsch," and many believe that "anything is art."

Being a freshly planted, exploratory, and curious thinker has its advantages, but finding ways to ground creative exploration in current events, upbringing, or other cultural traditions provides the surefooted start needed to proceed along a new course. Creativity theorists Peter Frensch and Robert Sternberg point out that we cannot move our thinking beyond a subject if we don't know where the subject exists to begin with. On the other hand, focused and entrenched knowledge about a field can result in a closed perspective that does not encourage a person to view problems any differently than she or he has in the past.[4] Originality, exoticism, otherness...none of these can exist without a standard from which to deviate.

Another rule-based standard is one of application. Most first-year students do not have the skill sets to carry out their ideas, so it is important for them to learn that every material has particular properties that must be handled in particular ways to achieve a particular effect. Nonetheless, no matter the discipline, the standards for superior, sufficient, or inadequate application are transferable. Good film editing is the same thing as precision woodworking, which is the same thing as designing elegant spatial proportions, which is no different from testing appropriate material strength or even using proper grammar when writing. Once we become accustomed to the idea that applications have constant and variable standards (and it could take a lifetime!) we are better able to get out of our own way and let the materials communicate with our instincts to experiment.

The other constant in the work of art and design is a willingness to break the rules once they are understood—maybe even those that we establish for ourselves. Our current K–12 education systems are disserving students since creative problem solving and its potential for failure have no place in a world that recognizes achievement through grades and assessment. The compulsion to work for a grade follows students into college, and I find that they feel pressured to imagine a polished, finished product that they can work toward rather than allowing themselves to venture someplace unexpected. They frequently tell me that they don't know what I want, as if their solutions should be based upon my needs. In response, I remind them that what I want is for them to think, which will involve more questions than answers at this point and will likely lead them someplace that I could not imagine for them—and could potentially lead them nowhere. I continually remind my students: "This is your research. Learn from it. Your work begins after you graduate." Better yet, print out this advice from Samuel Beckett and tape it over your desk: "Ever tried. Ever failed. No matter. Try again. Fail again. Fail better."

Recognizing that rules and systems—scientific, social, spiritual, and so on—govern all behavior, the consequences of breaking them and combining unlikely behaviors expands exponentially. A person adept at creative problem solving can enter most situations and find a way to resolve them with whatever is at hand.[5] In fact, I have often thought that being an artist or designer is the most difficult job in the world because in order to reflect upon or react against the human condition, an artist or designer must not only know her or his specific discipline but know something about everything else as well. It is difficult if not impossible to try to quantify the malleable and indeterminate processes of creative problem solving and critical making. Regardless, building on the complex context of possibilities, uncertainty, failure, and rules obeyed and broken, here are a few practical lessons that may lay the groundwork for what is possible in a Foundation course of study, along with examples to see what might come of them.

Lesson #1: Begin by looking at options, which is different from acting at random.

Thinking back to that native explorer, consider that preparation and planning lead to positive results. You won't be ready to address possibilities (and might not see them) without knowing your objective and being conscious of what it is asking of you. This is true for all working artists and designers. We don't sit around and wait for a jolt of imagination to jar us into action, or hope for a spark of genius. As the artist Chuck Close said: "Inspiration is for amateurs. The rest of us show up and get to work."[6]

Knowing how to make something involves tactile interaction with materials and substances, and making something innovative requires eye-hand processing that trains the brain as well. If you don't know what it is or how to do it, test it first. If your process is unclear at the beginning, try to envision possibilities for what could be revealed. Make sketches and models and impose variations on your approach. Although going someplace unexpected is a goal, the ability to apply calculated predictions to the route will lessen the chance of an undesirable destination.

An example from my "Studio Design" course shows how testing options can lead to something remarkable. After reviewing the cognitive "malfunctions" that occur when one's perception and conception do not align, students were asked to create a visual illusion. At first glance, it may appear that Daniel Cho's (BFA 2015 Industrial Design) point-of-view illusion involving a shadow (fig. 2) is the result of spontaneously arranged dormitory and cafeteria refuse. In fact, Daniel equipped himself for this expedition by beginning with a basic plan. A poster hanging in his dorm room served as the general map for a goal positioned loosely in his mind. With the help of a stable, fixed light source for reference, he was able to accumulate, arrange, and alter plastic utensils, cut paper, chopsticks, and even a wall clock into a delicately cantilevered and sophisticated table sculpture. Every material and action that went into the installation had to be precisely considered in response to what preceded it, and the finished assembly could not have been determined from the start.

Lesson #2: Learn to see by thinking more complexly about visibility.
Vision and its connection to perception and cognition is a troublesome and fascinating subject since it encompasses far more than physical or sensory function. Learning how vision and thought affect our seeing and understanding is indispensible for a student of art and design, as it would be for a student of science and any other problem-solving discipline. Each week in my "Studio Design" course I orchestrate exercises that force distinctions

Robert Doisneau
Les Musiciens devant Paris, 1957

between the collection of visual material (such as how we visually select, simplify, and compare elements) and its context (including placement and memory). These exercises emphasize that to see clearly, we must not only look more closely at visual objects and images, but also learn to imagine and interpret what is not visibly present.

To introduce a problem relating to scale, I asked my students to consider the invisible with regard to the impossibly small (microscopy) and the impossibly large (cosmology). Working with microscopes in the Nature Lab, students are encouraged to look at parts of themselves—their skin, fingerprints, hair, and fibers from their clothing—in ways that they have not done before. They record what they see in their sketchbooks, allowing the imagination to take over whenever necessary. I put forth no strict agenda for how they should respond to the question: "How can you map yourself through time and space using scale as a form of measure?"

Among a variety of responses, one solution spoke to the essence of vision as a process of understanding rather than an isolated act. Anthony Dahut's (BFA 2015 Furniture Design) six-foot-wide video projection showed a faintly off-color black-and-white scene with a nostalgic, home-movie quality (fig. 3). It looked like a field of untouched snow covered with a thin, crystalline glaze of ice. An eerie, uncomfortable shadow was cast from outside of the frame, and letters were slowly being formed in the snow. Although there was no way to see how the letters were being created, my thought was that this had been shot as a stop animation with some kind of liquid being poured onto the surface of the snow. The video ran through a few sequences of writing and drawing, which included Anthony's Social Security number, his address, and a self-portrait. When the lights came up, we could see a row of black boards and a black pen handle directly below where the video had been projected. Closer inspection revealed that each black board had a tiny fleck of white paper mounted to it, showing a microscopic view of the drawings in the video. What we were watching was not snow at all! Peering through the microscope, Anthony had discovered that he could push a small amount of

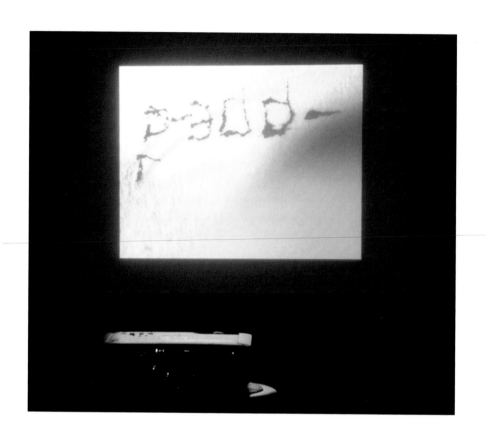

ink around with a strand of his hair, which he had fashioned to the end of a pen handle. He captured images of this process through the microscope, resulting in an animation of text and drawings.

Lesson #3: Use everything that you know and record everything.

In order to invite discovery, creative discourse must bridge multiple areas of interest and fields of study. Only one tool that I know of keeps diverse ideas, research, and reflection in one place so that they can smash together when you aren't paying attention: the sketchbook. However it is used, a sketchbook is the essential resource for recalling how one saw the world, interpreted a thought or observation, or projected imagination into possibilities for future investigations. Embracing a regimen for making and securing ideas so that they exist beyond the firing of the thought may well be the factor that distinguishes between creative types and critical makers.

I stress the importance of maintaining an active archive of ideas in a sketchbook from the outset of the Foundation experience, and types and variations of recording are folded into the first problem that I present in my "Studio Design" course. The problem, in short, asks that students go into the city and see with senses not yet dimmed by familiarity (as almost all of my students are new to the city when they arrive). Observations gathered from seeing, hearing, smelling, and even straining the body are to be recorded, then brought together in a work that expresses what it means to be here and now using the constructs of *progression* and *movement*.[7]

When Anna Riley (BFA 2014 Glass) arrived as a freshman, she brought with her a deep interest in science, including its ineffable brushes with philosophy and spirituality, and she was already an avid sketchbooker. Her sketches revealed paracosmic inventions that dabbled in astronomy and physics, so an exploration of the city piqued her highest curiosities. Intrigued by the interference, obstruction, and reflection of light sources coming from particular windows around the city, she visited their locations several times during the week to chart the cardinal directions and light angles throughout

Fig. 3
Anthony Dahut,
First Person, Singular
(installation view
and detail), 2012

the cycles of the day. Her records—drawings, notations, and imagined configurations—culminated in an installation of 12 pedestals, each representing a different building or different spots within the same building. A light mounted to a rotating arm traveled in an arc above the platforms, referencing the movement of the sun. The Plexiglas windows cast shadows that became living drawings, plotting along a grid noted with the time of the day and the locations in space (fig. 4). Without question, Anna's fruitful collection of ideas and observations allowed her to play with a concept to arrive at a presentation with great intellectual and technical merit.

Lesson #4: Don't try to get to the end without taking all the steps necessary to get there.

The final problem in my "Studio Design" course is complex; it encompasses several weeks of exercises, presentations, readings, and research just to arm students with the criteria that they need to set the standards of relevancy for solving the problem. Still, it never fails that some students approach me within minutes of reviewing the problem outline to ask if their immediately formed concept is acceptable. I tell them, "You can't know the answer yet. You haven't put your ideas to the test or pushed them through any options!"

I've learned to instruct students to dangle the final goal somewhere out of their reach and vision, not like a carrot on a stick in front of them but as if it might be suspended over their head. Always keep the goal in mind, but not as a destination. Keep it as a guide. You do not need to move toward it. In fact, you may need to pull away entirely and go in another direction, but the objective will remain with you. Those who are willing to just start making something no matter where those steps are leading will go much farther than those who timidly walk a direct line, because every step of the journey amounts to something.

The students are asked to create a game inspired by a work of art or design that they have viewed in person with the class, focusing specifically on the color palette. In preparation, we look extensively at color theories

Fig. 4
Anna Riley, *Set in the City* (details), 2010

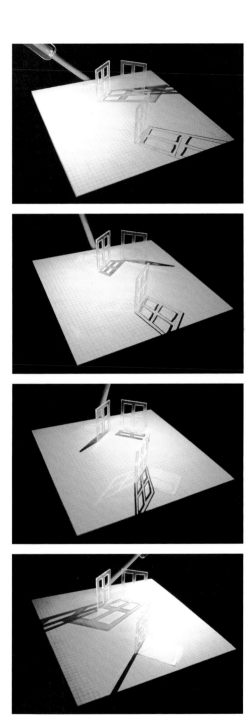

throughout history and across disciplines, including a viewing of Josef Albers's monumental *Interaction of Color* portfolio and his subsequent *Formulation: Articulation* portfolios in the Library Special Collections. Eun Sang (Ernie) Lee (BFA 2015 Furniture Design) was moved by Albers's work. He wanted to create a visual game based on the same aspects of color interaction that Albers was engaged with, but the similarities stopped there. Ernie abandoned Albers's rational, geometric compositions in favor of a gestural camouflage that was possibly influenced by his training in traditional Korean sumi brush painting. In Ernie's game, color swatch cards are placed behind trap doors, and players must determine matches between subtle hues even though the surrounding ground fools the eye into seeing slight variations in the colors (fig. 5).

While Ernie's first-year piece was thoughtfully conceived and carefully executed, it was not until later as a junior Furniture Design major that his curiosities about color interaction, gesture, geometry, and compartmentalization expanded. His cabinet exemplifies that every project we undertake builds upon that which came before it, and that nothing worthwhile can be achieved in a short amount of time with the least amount of steps (fig. 6).

Lesson #5: Understand that what you are learning is not the same thing as what is being taught.

It is hard to convince a student—especially a freshman—that all of this is for them and not for a grade, a teacher, a parent, or a job. Most of the things they learn won't be labelable, and they probably won't recognize that learning is taking place. I often partake in informal, verbal evaluations at the end of the course by asking students: "What is the most important thing that you learned in this class?" After a long silence as each of them searches for the answer that will earn them an *A*, I am always surprised by their answers. Once, an insightful young man blurted out: "That the food pyramid is not real."[8] If successful teaching and learning of critical thinking are measured by the re-establishment of a student's belief structures and assumptions

Figs. 5 and 6
Eun Sang (Ernie) Lee,
Color Play, 2008;
Untitled, 2011

while underpinning or replacing them with knowledge gained either by empirical techniques, logical reasoning, or abstract comparison, then this student's answer exceeded my greatest hope.

As teachers of aspiring artists and designers, we do little more than allow our students' experiences to be mediated through a critical stance based upon the definitions, theories, and demands of art and design as they exist within our concept of society. Somehow, we have come to be in this place at this time as an assortment of individuals for the sake of our experiences, understandings, and curiosities to explore topics in ways that we could not have considered before this gathering took place. And, with every new accumulation of individuals, none of us has any idea where our interactions will lead. Year after year, I remain completely unable to explain how any of this happens, but I have a great deal of faith that my students get it—whatever *it* is. Whether it occurs during my course, the following year, or five years down the road, this is where they learn to identify and sort through possibilities with confidence and initiative, and begin to discern what they can do and how it can impact their lives and the lives of others.

Notes

1. See T. M. Amabile, *Awakening Genius in the Classroom* (Alexandria, VA: ASCD, 1983); R. J. Sternberg, "The Theory of Successful Intelligence," in *Review of General Psychology* 3; and R. J. Sternberg and E. L. Grigorenko, *Teaching for Successful Intelligence* (Arlington Heights, IL: Skylight, 2000).

2. I only recall the casual reading of this metaphor, but it changed the way I thought about creativity.

3. Ian Hodder, "Creative Thought: A Long-term Perspective," in *Creativity in Human Evolution and Prehistory*, Steven Mithen, ed. (London: Routledge, 1998), 62.

4. P. A. Frensch and R. J. Sternberg, "Expertise and Intelligent Thinking: When Is It Worse to Know Better?" In R. J. Sternberg, ed., *Advances in the Psychology of Human Intelligence*, vol. 5 (Hillsdale, NJ: Erlbaum, 1989), 157–182.

5. I recall an episode at an artist residency years ago when the groundskeeper spent the entire day trying to retrofit his backhoe with a new front-end loader. He was a spry, capable, sun-hardened man whose stature revealed a life of physical labor, but wrestling with the misaligned coupling on the equipment was getting the best of him. I stopped by with another resident, artist Andrew Ginzel, to see what was going on, and after assessing the situation for a few minutes, Andrew put on the welding mask, took the torch from the groundskeeper, and proceeded to complete the job while dressed in a silk shirt and khaki shorts. That was cool.

6. Joe Fig, *Inside the Painter's Studio* (New York: Princeton Architectural Press, 2009), 42.

7. The criteria for the problem are deliberately open so that I can ascertain what a student already knows and is capable of from the outset of the course.

8. We had discussed the food pyramid in an earlier class in relation to systems of organization and hierarchies. A common visual tool for organizing the kinds and amounts of food necessary for a nutritional diet, the food pyramid's guidelines—initially developed by the National Dairy Council and the Meat Board—have been challenged by scientific communities.

Text and Context: Outward in All Directions

Daniel Cavicchi

How does a RISD education support the formation and
illumination of a meaningful "context" around and within
the "text" of works of art and design? In part through
its robust Liberal Arts curriculum, which both cultivates deep
learning in the humanities and fosters essential, integrated
interplay between studio and seminar. Daniel Cavicchi,
Dean of Liberal Arts, explores the inextricable connections
between any artwork and its social and historical surroundings,
highlighting examples in which such connections are
profound expressions of critical and ethical thinking.

Musicologist Charles Seeger once explained that in order to best understand his paper on the "unitary field theory of music," one had to begin in the middle and "then work outward in all directions."[1] Seeger was being provocative, suggesting connections between music and the broader realms of speech, behavior, and culture. However, as someone who spent much of his career working to escape the confines of formal analysis, he was also pointing to alternative ways in which one might derive meaning from an encounter with any single work, or text. The conventional way to read a text—from beginning to end—allows the text's structure to shape the reading experience and its meaning. We thus typically locate meaning "in" the text. Beginning at its middle and moving outward in all directions, however, defies this convention and reveals how any text and its meaning is always immersed in, and even constituted by, wider and more diverse *contexts*.

While most people oppose "text" and "context," the terms actually derive their meanings in relation to one another. The Latin "textus" refers to a "thing woven"; "context" refers more generally to a "joining together." Textual thinking addresses one's perception of the interrelated elements of physical form, emphasizing the fixed coherence of a work, something we name definitively with words like "object," "performance," or "design." Contextual thinking addresses a work more processually, highlighting not the fact of *coherence* but the more open-ended act of *connecting*, recognizing emergent and simultaneous domains of meaning that blur the boundaries of a text with its myriad settings—personal, social, political, historical, and so on.

Making, encountering, criticizing, and experiencing art would ideally entail a balanced use of these different frames of understanding. The problem, as Seeger suggested, is that texts have attained an extraordinarily exalted status in the discourse of Western art. From the Romantics of the eighteenth century, who insisted on "art for art's sake" in divorcing poetry from its surrounding social context, to the primacy of "the work" in much literary, music, and art criticism of the twentieth century, context has been undervalued as a generative and meaningful force in cultural expression.

Writers, composers, and artists achieve recognition and praise for their inno-vative texts rather than their innovative uses of context. Museum curators collect objects and exhibit them in display cases for the public; visitors do not come to galleries to see contexts. Our laws about expression are explic-itly text-based. Copyright law protects works "fixed in a tangible medium of expression" but does little to protect incorporeal traditions or values.

It hasn't always been this way. In other times, and in other cultures, the connections between social and historical contexts and cultural expression have been openly acknowledged, and texts have operated less as closed-off worlds of meaning than as fluid forms of public interaction and memory. In traditional, or "folk," communities, for example, songs or poems are often created from shared motifs, phrases, and means of assembly, or they are understood as emerging directly from particular conditions and circum-stances. Among the Kaluli of Papua New Guinea, song does not come from individual craft as much as the rich sonic environment of the rainforest; singers and performers have a deep metaphysical connection with the sound of water and birdsong.[2] The Tiv of Nigeria believe that any song's emotional meaning or "content" depends solely on who sings it and why. While West-ern ideologies of music locate happiness or sadness in the structure of major and minor scales, the Tiv would argue that a song is happy when it is sung at a birth and sad when it is sung at a funeral.[3] In American blues, songs freely borrow and repeat the same lines, melodies, and rhythms rooted in the col-lective experience of African Americans. As Muddy Waters once admitted about his song "Country Blues" (1941), whose motifs literally echo previous songs by Robert Johnson and Son House, among others, "This song comes from the cotton field."[4]

Questioning the overvaluation of textuality in artistic practice was pre-cisely the point of several avant-garde art movements of the twentieth cen-tury. Futurists and Dadaists, for instance, purposely highlighted the power of context in any artwork's creation and meaning by taking manufactured objects out of their everyday contexts and putting them into the refined worlds of the concert hall and gallery. Thus, Luigi Russolo established "The Art of Noises" in his 1913 manifesto and began composing music featuring machine guns and newspaper bellows onstage, and Marcel Duchamp scandalized the art world in 1917 by putting a mass-produced urinal on exhibit. In the 1960s, a range of provocateurs similarly challenged textual power: Roland Barthes declared the "death of the author," calling the novel "a tissue of quotations drawn from the innumerable centers of culture"; classical pianist Glenn Gould stopped performing live and advocated for the creativity of "dial twiddling" among stereo listeners; Andy Warhol appropriated the widely available commercial packaging of soup cans and soap boxes as his own.[5]

Even re-examinations of institutionalized art practices by a number of social scientists have emphasized the social context of creativity. Sociologist Howard Becker, for example, has argued that all artists and designers necessarily work in communities (or as he says, "artworlds") composed of suppliers, tool-makers, technicians, critics, and all others who collectively make *making* possible. Jason Toynbee, drawing on the theories of sociologist Pierre Bourdieu, has taken this argument a step further in claiming that all creative intentions and decisions are supported, constrained, and negotiated by a complex mixture of artists' dispositions; established practices, forms, and codes; and the likely fit between the two. He argues that professional, aesthetic, practical, and moral ways of thinking and doing define, in the broadest sense, a creative field of "possibles" that, in turn, enable what a creator might do.[6]

Making sense of the relationship of "text" and "context" is essential to the work of art and design, but how, exactly, are the issues and debates made concrete in art and design education? At first glance, Rhode Island School of Design reproduces the dominance of textual thinking in Western culture. RISD is a place where students are developing their own creative capabilities as professional artists and designers, learning how to use their own hands to craft diverse materials into objects. Walking around campus, one primarily sees students working with their bodies at easels, drafting desks, kilns, saws, and machines, and lots of *things* propped, pinned, piled, strewn, and hung. Yet contextualizing is always there. In expressive arts such as painting, ceramics, or sculpture, context is often fairly subjective. While most artists consider their work a contribution to society and social discourse, they frequently draw on personal experiences of the world as sources, trusting that unknown audiences will share their interests or appreciate their perspectives. In design fields such as architecture, graphic design, or industrial design, context is often made explicit in the creative process. Designers make things *for* particular people, places, and situations, whose qualities and meanings they study in order for their designs to be most relevant.

For both art and design students, contextual thinking has long been considered a vital aspect of education and practice at RISD. As early as 1901, RISD students in early architecture and modeling programs were required to take courses in art history and English; an agreement allowing students to enroll in courses at Brown University was made in 1903. In the 1930s, when the school began granting its first degrees, two years of English study were required, and a wide range of courses in art history, economics, French, history, physics, and public speaking were added to the curriculum. By 1940, a Division of Liberal Arts was established to organize this expanded realm of study. In 1956, leaders of the college specifically cited the importance of the humanities in training students for leadership in their fields and modified RISD's degree requirements to create a balance between students' "general education" and professional study.[7] RISD president John R. Frazier wrote that "Rhode Island School of Design's Division of Liberal Arts is dedicated to the development of responsible and responsive personalities, without which design education is not only futile but may even be socially unjustifiable."[8] These were strong words, pointing to the kind of artists and designers RISD valued. In fact, it evoked the origins of liberal arts in ancient Greece and Rome, where the study of the arts and philosophy comprised skills and attainments that were neither mechanical nor mundane but rather enabled free men to participate fully in public life.

Liberal arts is today one of the major categories of "arts" offered at RISD, along with design and fine arts. RISD undergraduate students take a full third of their classes in the liberal arts, across a variety of subjects, including archaeology, anthropology, art history, creative writing, history, literature, natural sciences, philosophy, psychology, religion, and sociology. The courses emphasize not only disciplinary education but developing makers who are critical, ethical, and articulate, and are wide-ranging enough to provide an exciting new set of "possibles" to a young artist or designer.

"Possibles" is a good word here, because *how* a student understands and integrates liberal arts study can take many different forms. For Adam Gault (BFA 1999 Film/Animation/Video) and Stefanie Augustine (BFA 1999 Illustration), for example, classes in American history and popular culture became an enriching subject for their work. Adam and Stefanie, working together after graduating, combined their artistic talents with their enthusiasm for American history to create an extraordinary animation of Lincoln's 1863 "Gettysburg Address." Through motion graphics and editing techniques, they vividly demonstrated and explained the funereal circumstances of the Address, the details of the Civil War's devastation, and the wider social issues that motivated Lincoln's resolve. Their dynamic and artful sensibility brought to life an antiquated and overanalyzed speech by emphasizing its poetic rhythms and liberating its meanings with abstract visual cues (fig. 7).[9]

Seth Snyder (BFA 2008 Industrial Design), concerned that the auditory was always made secondary to the visual in industrial design, took courses in music and science, and, as part of his degree project, read about the history of acoustics, the science of hearing, and cultural ideologies of sound. He decided to work with the visually impaired to explore how sound could function as a means of making sense of the world. After conducting observational

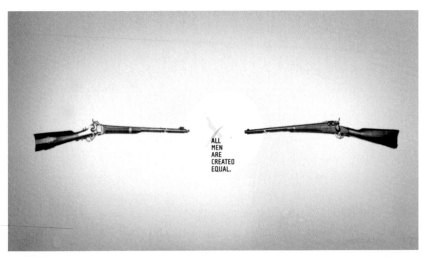

ALL
MEN
ARE
CREATED
EQUAL.

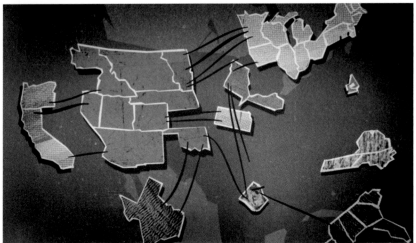

and interactive research with children and adults at the Perkins School for the Blind in Boston, and experimenting with his own "blind walks" in Providence, he combined his reading with such field experiences to think through ways in which he might improve the sensory awareness of the people he'd met. The result was a new walking cane for the blind that combined ultrasonic sensors and grip vibration to heighten the role of the auditory and the tactile in everyday navigation (fig. 8). After graduation, Seth started to think of himself not simply as a designer, but as a "design researcher," exploring deep connections between disciplinary practices of science, history, fieldwork, and design.[10]

Margaret Kearney (BFA 2013 Textiles) built on her commitment to environmental activism by taking classes in history, philosophy, and literature that addressed ecological issues, social justice, and theories of nature, and declaring a concentration (RISD's "minor") in environmental studies. Rather than writing policy or conducting scientific studies, she started to explore the ways in which she might apply her growing academic knowledge about environmental issues specifically in her work. The results include *Quilt for a New Community*, a colorful Midwestern friendship quilt subtly altered with black pieces of cloth representing the potentially dangerous flow of oil that would pass through America's heartland upon Congressional approval of the

Fig. 7
Adam Gault and
Stefanie Augustine,
*The Gettysburg
Address* (stills), 2010

Fig. 8
Seth Snyder on
a "blind walk" in
Providence, 2008

controversial Keystone Pipeline.[11] *Corn Stories*, a series of print designs, uses shifts in color and pattern to highlight corn's role in the history of the Midwest's landscape and agriculture. *Weaving Detroit*, a set of interior fabric panels, employs repeating images of male figures in a boardroom, planned buildings, and irregular, moss-like interruptions in the fabric to subtly suggest both the futuristic promise and degrading effects of the auto industry's presence in Detroit (fig. 9).[12]

Michael Mergen (MFA 2011 Photography) documented unusual polling places during an election year, many of them in makeshift spaces like shopping malls and bowling alleys. He soon focused on other spaces of citizen participation in democracy, such as jury deliberation rooms, National Guard recruitment offices, and halls used for naturalization ceremonies (figs. 10 and 11). In each project, he realized an incongruity between the ideals of our political system and the mundane realities of the spaces' furnishings and layout. To learn more about the history of citizen participation in democracy in the United States, he began talking to historians on campus and set up an independent study in which he read everything from Alexis de Tocqueville's perceptions of American democracy in the 1830s to theories about consumerism and the "public sphere" in the Great Depression to the changing meanings of the National Mall in Washington. Through this work, his photo series took on new significance and meaning, suggesting a "staging of democracy," which he too was enabling through his photographs.[13]

One of the most meaningful instances of contextual thinking for me as an instructor has been the Witness Tree Project, an ongoing collaborative model for teaching and learning developed in conjunction with the National Park Service (NPS). Witness trees are long-standing trees that have "witnessed" key events, trends, and people in American history. The project arranges for fallen witness trees to be shipped from NPS sites to RISD, where, in a joint history seminar (taught by me) and furniture studio (taught by Dale Broholm, a faculty member in Furniture Design), students interpret the history the tree "witnessed" and make relevant objects from the tree's wood.

Fig. 9
Margaret Kearney,
Weaving Detroit, 2012

The circumstance of working with the actual material of an historic tree is a powerful means for evoking the past and also for exploring design practice. In the course's history seminar, students learn not only about the events radiating from a tree's location—Theodore Roosevelt's reshaping of presidential power at his "summer White House" in Oyster Bay, New York, for example—but also about how a given tree poses questions of interpretation. To what extent can a tree serve as material evidence for American history? In the studio portion of the course, students make objects in ways that explicitly emphasize historical research and inquiry as a means for creation. Using hallowed wood from a particular landscape, they design objects informed by, and commenting on, themes and issues from the history of the tree's site and about which they have thoroughly read, discussed, and argued. Their design work is thus deeply situated, both figuratively and literally.

In the first year of the Witness Tree Project, we worked with the Hampton National Historic site, a former plantation outside of Baltimore, Maryland. The tree was a prize pecan, planted by Eliza Ridgley, the wife of John Ridgley, a notoriously disciplined slave master. After making an initial field trip to the historic site, where we saw the tree's former location and toured both the Ridgley mansion and grounds, some students realized that the interpretation of the site was dominated by the grand story of the Ridgleys, leaving the hardship of slaves' lives rather vague. Determining the appropriate emphasis for the various people that shaped Hampton's history became an important theme in class discussions and research. Given the richness of the artifacts in the Ridgley family home, as well as the absence of historical artifacts for the hundreds of slaves that lived there during its heyday, how might one accurately tell the story of the place for the public? How, exactly, should one render the painful story of slavery for visitors who might be more attracted to the story of the Ridgleys? What meanings could students justifiably draw from the wood of the pecan tree planted by the plantation's mistress?

Students researched and wrote papers about the broad theme of social identity in the antebellum South, including everything from leisure among

Figs. 10 and 11
Michael Mergen,
*Jury Room 706, Tulsa,
OK*, from the series
"Deliberate," 2010;
*Ceremony Room
#1, New York, NY*,
from the series
"Naturalization," 2011

the wealthy to abolitionism. Some commented on the increase in wealth and luxury goods among Maryland elites, researching the lives of slave-owning families and making such objects as an ornamented writing desk and a series of leisure games. Others, however, made objects that attempted to raise the profile of those traditionally de-emphasized in the Hampton story. Brittany Bennett (BFA 2011 Textiles), in order to balance the emphasis on dolls and toys in the Ridgley children's bedrooms, created a homemade-looking wooden doll from the pecan wood, dressing it in scraps of cloth that a slave girl might have saved (fig. 12). Rebecca Manson (BFA 2011 Ceramics) created a rough wooden stool that a slave might have used, giving it multiple legs of varying lengths and suspending tiny bells from the bottom of the seat, recalling an elaborate bell system that the Ridgleys used to call slaves to various parts of the house. The uneven legs cause an instability that rings the bells continually, symbolizing a slaves' inability to ever rest (fig. 13).

From the Theodore Roosevelt National Historic Site, the National Park Service offered us wood from several cherry and silver maple trees that had been planted shortly after Roosevelt's death; soon thereafter, the Park Service added a small quantity of wood from the George Washington Birthplace National Monument. After considering what those trees may have "witnessed" historically, I decided that the project for that year would focus on the memorialization of presidents in American life, something that could encompass everything from George Washington's teeth in the Smithsonian to the proliferation of presidential libraries. Running with this theme, one of the students, Felicia Hung (BFA 2013 Furniture Design), created a memorial bench, to be placed at the site between two cherry trees the Japanese gave to Roosevelt after he negotiated an end to the Russo-Japanese War in 1903. The bench commemorated Roosevelt's work by artfully bringing together two distinct planks, cherry and maple, in the shape of an "L," which also encouraged a more intimate reaction between any two people sitting on it (fig. 14). This simple and elegant piece was well researched, conceptually astute, and beautiful. Its design joined together not only different species of

Fig. 12
Brittany Bennett,
Doll, 2009

Fig. 13
Rebecca Manson,
Polyrhythmic Stool, 2009

Fig. 14
Felicia Hung, *Treaty
of Portsmouth*, 2010

wood but also much of the intellectual work we had been doing in seminar on American history, presidential power, and public memory.

Henry Zimmerman (BFA 2013 Industrial Design) likewise summed up a semester of discussion and research on the complexities of Franklin D. Roosevelt's presidency when we worked with wood from the national historic sites of Franklin D. Roosevelt and Eleanor Roosevelt in Hyde Park, New York. Henry created a wheelchair that largely replicated the converted dining-room chair on wheels that FDR used in his home, but he replaced the chair's usual push handles with a large ship's wheel. Referencing FDR's celebration of the common as well as his fascination with maritime history, the multi-handled ship's wheel also suggested the complexity of his presidency during the Depression. FDR took the helm of the nation-state during a time of crisis, but he also depended on others for support, especially the First Lady, who both wheeled him around the house and counseled him on matters of social justice. The chair was thus complicated in its technical challenges and in its interpretive, embedded biographical and historical research.

The Witness Tree Project is a particularly explicit example of integrating liberal arts and studio learning, and I have learned a lot about differences and similarities among disciplinary discourses in the process of teaching it. Initially, I found myself struggling to apply evaluative measures common to the humanities—such as the persuasiveness of a thesis based on clarity, definition, and evidence, and how it might contribute to human knowledge—to students' designs. Yet as I observed students in the studio, developing their objects from initial brainstormed sketches and library research to the working-out of technical problems and final construction, I realized that the design process involved intense levels of academic work: drafting, testing, and feedback; thoughtful attention to meaning; and careful analysis and synthesis.

The differences are important to keep in mind, of course. A successful scholarly paper follows a clear sequence to make a persuasive argument. By contrast, a successful studio object often abides by very different principles of layering, suggestion, association, and provocation. John Dewey explained this as the difference between a statement, which one deciphers, and expression, which one experiences: "The poem, or painting, does not operate in the dimension of correct descriptive statement but in that of experience itself.... Prose is set forth in propositions. The logic of poetry is super-propositional even when it uses what are, grammatically speaking, propositions."[14] Linguist Roman Jakobson carried the distinction even further in the 1950s, noting that not only language but also human thought itself is framed by, on one side, the metonymic (exemplified by the contiguity of prose, in which one thing leads to another) and, on the other side, the metaphoric (exemplified by the simultaneity of poetry, in which one thing is juxtaposed with another).[15]

Despite these differences, at their core, liberal and studio arts are both processes of making. Here is Dewey again: "The odd notion that an artist does not think and a scientific inquirer does nothing else is the result of converting a difference of tempo and emphasis into a difference of kind."[16] Indeed, the more I have thought about it, object-making seems at least as well-suited for the practice of history as writing does. The relationship between objects and the past, after all, is a deep one; in history seminars, like the one in the Witness Tree Project, we make history by "reading" the past in old artifacts. In the Witness Tree Project studio, students make history, too, only they do so by "writing" the past into new objects. If anything, the Witness Tree Project aligns, to mutual benefit, the realms of creativity and scholarship. Students' designed objects, from historic wood, are literally shaped by historical analysis; their written historical analyses are honed by shaping wood hundreds of years old. Both acts of making are ultimately forms of animation, instilling with life materials and events that, otherwise, would likely be forgotten.

Charles Seeger helped to establish the Society for Ethnomusicology in 1955. The organization was, in many ways, a realization of Seeger's interest in "moving outward in all directions" from the musical text. The scholarly study of music in the 1950s was centered on the close analysis of the structure of musical works and the circumstances of the composers who created them. Ethnomusicology, however, challenged that approach by instituting the study of music in an *ethnos*, or culture. This didn't mean simply building historical or biographical understanding around musical works, offering new containers for songs or symphonies, but rather more fundamentally exploring how contextual understanding might affect what we call "music." Over the years, ethnomusicologists have left the very subject of their study open for debate, a history that might be summarized in changing conjunctions and reversals—"music *and* culture," "music *in* culture," "music *as* culture," "*music-culture*," "*culture* in *music*," and so on.

I realized this fundamental shift as a college student in the 1980s. I had been a classical music lover and a literature major deeply invested in the idea of great works and in close textual analysis. But after attending a lecture by ethnomusicologist Charles Keil, in which he situated Cuban music's rhythms into wider and wider frameworks of Cuba's politics and history, I realized that the structures of what I had known fundamentally as "music" were only sonic traces of the diverse people, attitudes, experiences, and forces that had brought those sounds into being and given them meaning. I stopped listening to "music" that day and started listening to the philosophies, technologies, and human history from which music emerges.

Contextual thinking in art and design is similar. When new students find themselves for the first time at RISD, a place where they can finally fully indulge their artistic sensibilities, they sometimes resent the pressure of having to continue the kind of academic work they felt forced to do in high school. "Why do I have to write an essay about the history of immigration? What does that have to do with art?" they ask. This reaction is understandable, but it also reveals a naive conception of "art" that assumes it comes from "within" and not from exploration, empathy, and experience. While they may not know it, the objects that emerge from this tiny toolkit are depressingly conventional. Once students understand how new experiences and connections might redefine their goals and practices—even if it's not always entirely comfortable—they have revelations. Margaret Kearney, the Textiles major and environmental activist, for example, found that her work in Liberal Arts made her re-think the very act of weaving: "Being an environmental studies concentrator, I've spent time learning about ways that the materials, processes, and social systems that are required for me to make my work are problematic.... I kept asking myself questions about whether making so much *stuff* was a valid use of time, questioning the purpose of making." At the same time, she found that her Liberal Arts courses have helped her "create work that's increasingly nuanced and specific" and "to bridge experiences that I've had outside of RISD doing activist work and my studio practice, serving as a means to process the experience through a conceptual framework."[17]

As a matter of course, contextual thinking develops for all RISD students as they progress through their degree requirements and accumulate experiences with disparate modes of learning. Such work requires them to negotiate multiple discourses and expectations as they move back and forth from seminar to studio. Engaging with depth and facility across multiple disciplinary approaches also requires a sharp awareness of divisions and overlaps in categories of thought. In the same way that researchers have suggested multilingual speakers develop a heightened ability in multi-tasking and memory, or that integrative learning requires particular creative problem-solving skills, RISD students, by the time they graduate, develop a familiarity with meta-thinking, which, in turn, heightens their ability to see new connections and meanings.[18]

Contextual thinking in art and design is thus literally transformative. We typically think of "transformation" as referring to change, which is true at a general level, but its Latin roots more precisely refer to a "forming across." This is exactly what artists and designers who think contextually do: They reconfigure forms across previously accepted categories of definition. Their art "moves" us, because they have moved the boundaries of our understanding. The cultural movements of which they are a part create change in society because they skillfully advance new frameworks of thought that reshape public discourse. Their reach in creating a "thing woven" thus leads us all to consider new possibilities for "joining together."

Notes

1. Charles Seeger, *Studies in Musicology, 1935–1975* (Berkeley: University of California Press, 1977), 103.

2. See Steven Feld, *Sound and Sentiment: Birds, Weeping, Poetics, and Song in Kaluli Expression* (Philadelphia: University of Pennsylvania Press, 1982).

3. Charles Keil and Steven Feld, *Music Grooves: Essays and Dialogues* (Chicago: University of Chicago Press, 1994), 162–163.

4. Siva Vaidhyanathan, *Copyrights and Copywrongs: The Rise of Intellectual Property and How It Threatens Creativity* (New York: New York University Press, 2001), 122.

5. See Roland Barthes, "The Death of the Author," *Aspen*, nos. 5 & 6 (1968); Glenn Gould, "The Prospects of Recording," *High Fidelity Magazine* 16, no. 4 (April 1966): 46–63; *Campbell's Soup Cans*, Museum of Modern Art, http://www.moma.org/collection/browse_results.php?object_id=79809.

6. Howard S. Becker, *Art Worlds* (Berkeley: University of California Press, 1982); Jason Toynbee, *Making Popular Music: Musicians, Creativity, and Institutions* (New York: Oxford University Press, 2000).

7. Albert E. Simonson, "Report on the Liberal Arts at RISD," *Rhode Island School of Design Alumni Bulletin* (May 1956): 15–16.

8. Press Release, Rhode Island School of Design, April 26, 1956.

9. The video can be viewed at http://adamgault.com/#/work/gettysburg.

10. Snyder discusses this project on his blog, *ThoughtLines*. See http://sethsnyder.net/projects/ambio-urban-navigator/.

11. Kearney won a prestigious Udall Scholarship for this project in 2012.

12. Kearney's work is featured at http://www.margaretkearney.com.

13. You can see the series that made up Michael Mergen's graduate thesis work at http://mimages.com.

14. John Dewey, *Art as Experience* (New York: Minton, Balch & Co., 1934), 84–85.

15. Roman Jakobson, "Two Aspects of Language and Two Types of Aphasic Disturbances," in *On Language*, Linda R. Waugh and Monique Monville-Burston, eds. (Cambridge, MA: Harvard University Press, 1990), 115–133.

16. Dewey, *Art as Experience*, 15.

17. Correspondence with the author, March 22, 2013.

18. On multilingualism, see David L. Wheeler, "Being Bilingual: Beneficial Workout for the Brain," *Chronicle of Higher Education*, February 20, 2011. Accessed online at http://chronicle.com/article/Being-Bilingual-Beneficial/126462/. Research on integrative learning is vast; for a helpful summary, see Ross Miller, "Integrative Learning and Assessment," *Peer Review* 7, no. 4 (2005): 11–14; or the articles at the Carnegie Foundation's Integrative Learning Project at http://gallery.carnegiefoundation.org/ilp/index.htm.

Conversation: Drawing

Patricia C. Phillips

How does drawing—a ubiquitous form of rendering images and ideas—serve and perform in twenty-first century art and design practice? Patricia C. Phillips, Dean of Graduate Studies, gathered five RISD faculty members—Silvia Acosta, Professor, Architecture; Cas Holman, Assistant Professor, Industrial Design; Daniel Lefcourt, Assistant Professor, Foundation Studies; Andrew Raftery, Professor, Printmaking; and Kevin Zucker, Associate Professor, Painting—to seek their perspectives on drawing in the world at large, in their disciplines, and in their teaching. Drawing emerged as experimental, iterative, and improvisatory, and the conversation, in turn, took surprising directions—dipping into chance and discovery, subversive teaching, and developing what Lefcourt calls an "ethics of making."

Drawing has a long history of representation that seeks to imitate through close observation and carefully contrived symbolic systems of lines and marks rendered objectively. Drawing also often elaborates on reality and happens intuitively. While the unfolding of the process itself can invite both analytical and abstract interpretation, for hundreds of years, drawings were expected and assumed to be a representation or interpretation of some thing, person, or place—"the miraculous conjuring of images from thin air."[1] But in the twentieth and twenty-first centuries, drawing has become a subject and process of exponentially expanding exploration, including images that emerge from imagination, the process of making, expository gesture, improvisational act, and diagrammatic explication. Today, drawing is a noun and a verb that is ubiquitous, partially proposed, or radically redone. Indeed, as Jean Fisher and Stella Santacatterini describe it, "The impulse to draw is not to capture appearance so much as a demand to animate thought. Thus drawing is always beyond perception, the other side of perception."[2]

Whenever in New York I faithfully go to the Drawing Center where, whether an exhibition is contemporary or historical, I am reliably immersed in questions about the "expanded field" of drawing.[3] For some 30 years, I have witnessed extreme virtuosity in the ambitious, ephemeral installations, striking material experimentation, and countless puzzlements of form or process. I witness the same discursive and generative approaches to drawing in the student work at RISD—in studios, galleries, incidental spaces, and occasionally while looking over the shoulder of a student drawing in her journal. Unless your eyes are closed, on any given day at RISD you will encounter evidence of the speculative, searching, whimsical, observational, abstract, obsessive, and projectively imagined in the form of drawing.

I was honored to share a conversation about drawing with five RISD faculty members, each representing a different history. Serving from one to 29 years at RISD, all are practicing artists or designers and committed and introspective teachers whose perspectives on drawing and teaching are as varied as their disciplines and subjectivities. Our conversation considers "the drawing," but what emerges is evidence that the process of drawing—its sometimes messy vitality, vulnerable contingencies, and temporal conditions of making—serves as a rich metaphor for a range of experimental, open-ended, or improvisatory activities. The restlessness and inherent inquiry of drawing serves as a striking surrogate for art itself, as well as for how we think about its dynamic and symbolic role in art and design teaching and pedagogy. Arguably, drawing is one of the best—and most companionable—resources to teach about and with, as well as a flexible instrument to make speculative forays into the future of art with the young women and men we are teaching. If I ponder Richard Serra's declarative aphorism, "There is only drawing," I unquestionably endorse that "there is drawing" at RISD that is profoundly connected, if not core, to its teaching and learning mission.

PATRICIA PHILLIPS This is a conversation about how we teach, utilize, and engage drawing as an action, idea, pedagogical resource, and vibrant metaphor. I expect there will be moments when we will be very focused on drawing at RISD. I also hope there will be expansive moments where we contextualize our work and address critical questions about art, design, and teaching.

Perhaps we should begin our conversation on drawing with how we understand it in the world at large. As you consider a historical trajectory of drawing, has there been significant rethinking about it in the past few decades, for example, given the expansion of digital media?

KEVIN ZUCKER I hate to start off on this note, but while the impact of drawing in early conceptualism, process art, and systems-based work in the twentieth century was significant, I think the growing market for collecting drawings in the past 30 years has changed things. What was a space for experimentation might now be the predominant art product.

ANDREW RAFTERY Yes, in contemporary art there is a huge part of the art market that is dedicated to elaborate works on paper as finished works. They are not exploratory necessarily—and generally not as interesting as many sketchy drawings.

SILVIA ACOSTA Can't an exploratory drawing also be a finished work?

AR I think so. Look at Raphael's or Michelangelo's exploratory drawings for painting, sculpture, or architecture. Part of the reason they are so compelling is that the artist had a question that was being asked while the drawing was being made. And the drawing was finished when the question was answered and it was time to go on to the next question.

DANIEL LEFCOURT What is it about drawing in relation to the rest of visual culture that has caused this surging market for drawings? Is it a coincidence that it has happened alongside the rise of the digital?

KZ Of course there's the fetishizing of touch that is partially in response to a world increasingly comprised of screens. I also think that there is an embrace of the provisional and related aesthetics.

PP Yes, there is something about a drawing that can be constructively conditional or contingent. It is often imperfect, half done, or redone. It can live in many spatial and temporal conditions. It can be spontaneously evocative or unfold over a prolonged period of time. Its ubiquity and inherent flexibility make drawing a tremendous resource, as well as something difficult to precisely define. Perhaps this partially explains our preoccupation with drawing at this very moment.

CAS HOLMAN I can't help but link the interest in drawing to the fact that cursive is no longer taught in many elementary schools. Many children are not learning to write script and, instead, often learn typing in third grade. And we're seeing fewer children taking art classes. People too often think that some people are "naturally" good at drawing—that it isn't something like mathematics that has to be learned and developed. Drawing is something that you learn. Forgive this example, but you're more likely to draw a perfect box in two-point perspective if you draw a thousand straight lines

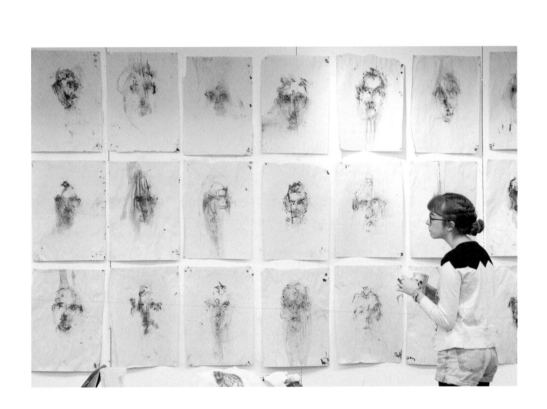

first. I think we're going to see that drawing itself as a product or work of art becomes more valuable as we drift further away from the opportunity or ability to draw.

PP   Moving from the big picture to RISD, can you characterize students' relationships to drawing? Having grown up with emergent digital technologies, are students passionate about drawing? I had a colleague (at another school) who taught drawing in an architecture program. He spent the first half of the semester only *talking* about drawing. For seven weeks, students were prohibited to draw in their drawing course! Finally, when they were permitted to draw, following this prolonged act of withholding, they had developed an almost desperate desire to draw. While I do not necessarily endorse this process, is there a sustained commitment to drawing at RISD?

AR   RISD's first-year Foundation Studies curriculum consistently helps students to discover how to use drawing to access something within themselves. When they come into the majors as sophomores, they have this drawing background, which allows them to work generatively and freely and to harness their creativity and imaginations (see fig. 15).

   Teaching drawing at this stage in Printmaking is getting them in touch with the idea that drawings are made in a particular way, with particular materials, and that drawing, and by extension all forms of making, is something that they do with their bodies. Foundation Studies relies a great deal on charcoal, erasing, and pressing and pressuring materials. When I teach students silver point, no matter how hard you press, it doesn't get darker and it cannot be erased. Or if I teach them how to make a quill pen from a feather, they cannot press hard or it breaks. They learn new ideas about content that are inherent in the materials themselves.

KZ   When I was an undergraduate at RISD myself, a big part of my indoctrination was the number of hours spent on the floor covered in charcoal and making marks—this idea of drawing as a heroic act.

Fig. 15
Drawing exercise
in the Painting
department

SA Drawing is physical. We can intuitively understand the consequences of pressure in mark-making: the sensing of the body, arm, and hand. I think this first-year exposure to drawing, which is so much a part of the fine arts, is incredibly valuable to teaching architectural drawing, where one has to choose critically what techniques to employ, what kind of materials to use, and what set of ideas to make visible. Historically, architecture exists in the academic environment through drawing. The more exposure students have to different drawing techniques, the more informed their choices can become.

DL Following Hurricane Sandy, I was unable to get out of Brooklyn for a week. I sent students a message: "Here's the assignment: Make a drawing. That's it. Let's see what happens." Students' interests started to register in different ways. Some just couldn't get enough of drawing, whereas others were more hesitant. Many first-year students aren't necessarily coming into RISD with deep drawing experiences. The students without much drawing background were reluctant to engage, whereas students who came to RISD having drawn a lot wanted to draw all the time.

SA Yes, if you haven't drawn extensively it's difficult. In the past 15 years or so, I find myself having to talk about the value of drawing because in practice it's becoming a little bit extinct. This is not just happening in the Department of Architecture at RISD, but in the discipline as a whole. Software and digital techniques produce amazing things, right? But the participation of the hand in exploring, thinking, and visual expression has a significant role in the design disciplines. I am trying to recuperate and preserve it, and I do think it can be brought back. There are now architectural firms seeking "digital painters" rather than software programs to produce their imagery. They want to see the evidence of the hand in all of its tentative expressions and decisions—rather than finite and absolute images produced by "straight-up" software.

CH Students come into Industrial Design and in the first month begin a rigorous drawing experience. We teach sketching as visualization—"rapid vis sketching." We use drawing as a way to find ideas and represent them, as a process of ideation that deepens learning. They go through two 200-foot rolls of paper, using only Sharpies (fig. 16). There's a collaboration between the act of drawing and whatever they can picture in their heads that is sorted out on paper, using the hand to figure out an idea.

This exercise challenges what a drawing is or what it does; it is not about creating a precious or finished product. Some students struggle with this approach. I'll often see their sketchbooks or journals filled with gorgeous drawings. They are comfortable with a particular kind of drawing and have to work to reconcile how it relates to this other type of process drawing.

AR I'm interested in drawings that have a function, that get an artist to another stage. I'm less concerned with drawing as the final result and much more interested in the work that drawing is doing. I would hope that this would be a model for how students engage other techniques or technologies so that they are not simply about an end product, but opportunities to get where they have to go as artists.

In my teaching I frequently use our museum. We look at drawings that are more than 300 years old. There's a sketch of St. Jerome with a certain amount of filling in and resolution. Right next to this is another drawing that is less developed. The students actually can see the decision-making—how the artist got it from one line or passage to the other because of the way the pen has been used on the paper. There is an immediacy that I don't think we would ever find in the more finished works of that period. We also look at other drawings from 200 years later and others from much closer to our time that offer similar insights. I try to employ a constructive nostalgia for how ideas and techniques are passed along. It is wonderful to look at beautiful drawings from the past, but the really exciting part is to see how the drawing reveals the thinking process of the original maker.

DL A consistent thread here is drawing as ideation, as a provisional and investigative process that is neither pressured nor pristine.

KZ We have to discuss distinct definitions too though, because different conceptions of drawing are strikingly evident at RISD. They're not consistent within or across departments. In fact, I think such differences are one of the principal characteristics of the school.

For my graduate drawing class in the Painting department, I define drawing as "anything that works in parallel to a student's primary practice." So, it can be photography or writing or performance. Whatever it is, it operates at some remove and can be more experimental. I think we all now start with the proposition that drawing can be art; we know it can be of equal value to painting. But I decided to pursue an antiquated idea of drawing as facilitating some other body of work. We talk extensively about what the two practices do and don't have to do with one another. It's never simply preparatory.

PP It's codependent.

KZ Yes, the idea of codependency is interesting. One thing I teach is to question the autonomy of individual art objects. The artist Peter Halley talks about exhibitions having replaced works as the basic integer of meaning—and things can be codependent even across two separate bodies of work.

SA I question whether drawing can be anything, any material, or any expression. I think that boundaries and self-limitations are useful and I'm actually more interested in the differences than the similarities between marks and processes. Recently in my drawing seminar some students challenged these boundaries, pushing drawing to cross the threshold into something else, like sculpture. One student brought in hanging string and called it a "drawing." To some degree I understood the impulse, but the lines were not marks made by the hand; it was an arrangement of a linear material. This presented a productive conflict that will help me clarify the way I write a problem in the future—to preserve mark-making as drawing versus selecting and arranging material in the form of an assemblage.

Fig. 16
Drawing exercise in
the Industrial Design
department

AR Would you consider an architectural model equivalent to a drawing?

SA No, I would not call a model a drawing. Even though both can be steps to clarify or arrive at a purpose, they don't provide the same information. Drawing is a tool that gets you somewhere. In the production of architecture, the act of drawing takes two forms: one is in the making of objective, calibrated marks in order to understand a space or set of instructions; the other is the making of subjective images that convey conceptual traces, experiential properties, and personal artistic expression (see fig. 17).

AR I also make distinctions. For example, I would never describe an etching as a drawing even though drawing skills are used in etching. Likewise, there is a significant difference between a lithograph and a drawing even though they look so much alike and many people confuse the two. I want students to think of a lithograph as a print that is different from a drawing. What comes first is the drawing that prepared us to do the print. The print invokes a different level of commitment to the image.

CH As I said, we have a reputation for rapid visualization; our students sketch throughout their four years. But I don't know that it's drawing. It's visualizing. At the same time, we make sketch models with paper that are more like drawing. We hack things together to imagine things in space. We sketch with prototypes. If I substitute the word "drawing" for "sketching" then a lot more of our processes, even down to experiments and research, are forms of drawing.

Fig. 17
Christine Zavesky,
Bridge Study, 2008

DL In my courses the question is: How do we apply speed, play, and improvisation to any material—graphite and paper, video, a three-dimensional object made out of clay or paper, or an image in Photoshop?

AR In my own work, I've started to make small sculptures of figures and foamcore models of settings. I consider these drawings in that they get me where I want to go, and I do teach this as a technique to my students; they

make forms and draw from them. I also think it is very important to introduce students to collage. In the twentieth century, collage was an important generative process for artists. For younger artists doing a lot of their work on computers using Photoshop, some experience with the physical, manipulated collage gives them critical insight on the digital process. I think in 20 years digital collage will be the art of our time. Artists are finding extraordinary ways to make images by manipulating them through computers, which might end up becoming the handmade paintings or sculptures of the future.

DL In Industrial Design, do you teach drawing on a tablet or is it all analog?

CH Well, they learn to use a tablet whether or not we teach it. Our students are proactive like that. By the time they graduate they all have software and digital-drafting skills, but we don't teach drawing as technical drafting anymore. For a rendering—a glamour shot—we often go back and forth between digital, the hand, and the three-dimensional model.

KZ Digital approaches to drawing are a significant part of my own practice. Someone once remarked to me that where we used to draw a square as four perpendicular, connected sides of equal length, now, in software, we drag a point diagonally from one corner to another to make a square.

AR An assignment that I use when we learn color in printmaking speaks to another kind of puzzle. One of the most difficult things to teach in color printmaking is the idea of making separate matrices and then putting them together to make all the colors you need. The impulse is to make an outline and fill it in with color. So, we have a setup in studio that has a full range of primary and tertiary colors. The students are given four sheets of acetate and four Sharpie markers in various colors. When they're drawing the yellow, they stay on the yellow piece of acetate. When they're drawing the red, they draw on the red piece of acetate. They use all four different acetates for the different colors and directly see how the whole thing adds up to a full image, full color. When they pull it apart, they see how abstract those shapes are and how they could never have figured it out without actually seeing it. Then they can transfer those images to their plates or stones and start to work in black. It helps them to make a breakthrough about printmaking.

PP Since RISD launched its five-year strategic plan last year, we have talked frequently about "critical making" as a philosophy, perspective, or sensibility particular to RISD. Is there a particular relationship between critical making and drawing?

AR In spite of our different departments and disciplines, we share the value of working with our hands and a deep commitment to object making. I often show a documentary on self-taught artist James Castle, who was profoundly deaf and had no language, but who drew so exquisitely using only fireplace soot and saliva. The film is about being an artist and the passionate necessity for making things.

CH I think that there's a difference between craft and making—and RISD has a rich tradition of making. What I like about drawing, sketching, and sketch models are how they relate to a process of discovery and invention—not craft.

DL Maybe it's about how to instill an ethics of making as opposed to developing a set of techniques. The technical-school model teaches students how to fulfill a specific, predefined role of what constitutes mastery. That's not what you do as an artist. What constitutes quality and excellence if what you are doing is no longer measurable against an ideal model? I think the alternative to the master model is teaching students how to learn for themselves. The fear many have regarding the loss of this master model is that now anything goes. But the real alternative is to teach students how to develop a practice, how to be an inventor, and then to guide them through the stages of development.

I heard about a figure drawing course at another school where students can only use triangles to articulate form, as training for creating 3-D models.

While interesting, this couldn't be more different from my own approach. In fact, I don't teach observational drawing to first-year students. All of the work is generated from making—from material or visual experimentation. The goal of drawing is to learn something.

PP Educator and theorist Henk Slager calls the process of art inquiry and research "nameless science."

CH Learning emerges from curiosity rather than trying to confirm something. When you set out to prove something, you're inclined to set up your test in a way that predetermines the outcome.

KZ Confirmation bias.

CH Right. This happens frequently with children. They are building with blocks and someone says, "What is that? What are you making?" The child thinks, "Okay, so it has to be a thing, and now I have to communicate what this thing is. It has to be something real because this person asking me these questions has to understand what it is." The framing of the question produces a response such as, "It's a building. A car. My house." But if the question is, "Can you tell me about what you're doing?" they'll answer, "Well, I'm stacking some stuff," or, "I'm making a giant giraffe monster spaceship." The framing of the question often perpetuates overly determined outcomes.

DL This is a key challenge in developing a curriculum or an art project. How do you build chance and discovery into a prompt and a process? I am curious if this is a specialty at RISD.

CH I try to fine-tune the balance of how much information to provide. It reduces anxiety when people know what's going on but, at the same time, if you tell them where something is headed it can limit what they're open to along the way.

KZ As a student in Foundation Studies, I had Ken Horii for 3-D design. He would give an assignment and everybody would ask: "Can we do this? Can it be made out of that?" At one point, he said, "The more questions you ask me, the more there are limits on your potential responses."

CH I have had good results with, "Just paper, just tape, just a pencil, and nothing else." They figure out how to make the tape a hinge and other fantastic things happen. Reggio Emilia—the Italian early childhood schooling based on free inquiry—teaches students to teach themselves by setting a stage or context for them to explore. Teachers, parents, and children are equal shareholders in learning initiatives. I think RISD has some of these affinities. We set a stage with specific prompts or tools and support their exploration. We have to have a very open mind for change and innovation because, by the time they graduate, we can't even imagine what they're going to need to know. They need to be able to navigate through change.

DL I try to walk the students through the process of invention using chance and unorthodox methods of discovery that can be fun or difficult or even emotionally wrenching. But there's always the nagging question, "When do we get down to business and hands-on skills?" There's a part of me that wants to say "never." You teach someone to teach herself and she develops the skills. And there's a part of me that says, "Actually, maybe we should do a technical exercise," to establish some foundation.

CH Sometimes I'll say, "Come up with 10 ways to light a room that don't involve electricity," or, "Come up with 20 ways of getting water from point A to point B." And they respond, "Well, I have a pelican and a sponge and my cupped hands, and there's the magnetic pull of the moon on water. What else can I do?" When they max out on thinking outside the object and want to throw things at me, I propose, "Okay, now we'll learn some Photoshop."

PP You narrow the conditions, create friction, and possibly some frustration. Kevin, I know that you've used the idea of obstruction in your courses.

KZ "The Five Obstructions" (inspired by Lars von Trier and Jorgen Leth's 2003 film) is an assignment I give to prompt students to question their assumptions and patterns. For a student who works very slowly, do it in five seconds. For a student who works very quickly, take a week to do it. These opposite approaches tend to draw out unexpected materials, process, color, and so on.

This question of predetermining outcomes connects to risk-taking and failure. At RISD, we rightly valorize failure, though this can become romantic. Pedagogically, when does an idea of risk or failure become an indulgence with an established—and conforming—set of aesthetics? Yet I am still interested in what happens when a material meets some force and disruption occurs.

PP Education theorist Neil Postman wrote many books, but two resonate with me as we talk. The first is *Teaching as a Subversive Activity*, with Charles Weingartner in 1969. Ten years later, he wrote *Teaching as a Conserving Activity*. Thinking about the subversive-conserving dialectic, can someone talk more about how drawing in particular might serve those pedagogical goals?

AR Obsolete technology has become a cultural preoccupation. Students have an interest in cinematography, for example, that is so arduous and so unlikely. In my drawing class, when I show them how to make ink from oak galls that we grind up, strain, and mix with ferrous sulfide, then use that ink to draw with goose quills, I'm really surprised by what good sports they are. They are eager to learn information and solid skills so that they can create their own techniques and processes in the future. I do think that a part of what we do as teachers is stewardship of certain skills and ways of working that we embody and pass along. I know that I have learned things that our students will not learn unless I teach them. I think that's part of our mission in education. It's not all about always creating new knowledge.

CH I have heard that there is a RISD professor who's infamous for tearing students' drawings off the wall. This has prompted some great conversations with students about critique and pedagogy. What's good for one person is terrible for another. In my field, what's good for the six-foot-tall person is terrible for someone in a wheelchair. In the end, I think that the relationship between a teacher and a student involves trust. The narrative is something like, "I suggested that you to try something and you did. It worked out and that's great because I wasn't sure it would."

AR When I was in art school, teachers drew on our drawings. It was very disconcerting. I go to the studio with a small pad and draw for the students to demonstrate different ways things look or approaches on how to see things—accuracy, proportions, qualities of line—more clearly.

CH Conserving and subverting invokes an internal tension in teaching—and perhaps drawing is a metaphor for this. When students come into Industrial Design, we have to reprogram their thinking about products, sort of wean them off the shiny objects. So, I think that the process of sketching, sketch modeling, and spending so much time with process is a first step toward what I value or would like to see, not just in my teaching but in the industry I teach for.

PP I hear and observe all of the time that RISD students have an amazing work ethic and that they're very disciplined. I'm interested in how this might relate to qualities of drawing.

DL In Foundation Studies the work ethic and the expectations are established immediately. Before the students meet the faculty, they've been told, "Get ready. You're about to work a lot." I don't know how all of this social engineering developed, but it works.

CH RISD students' work ethic is simple—they want to be awesome. They work hard because they want to learn, explore, and be great designers.

PP It's not only about becoming a leader in your field, it's an advanced and persistent sense of inquisitiveness, which might find expression in drawing.

CH Yes, you ask for 10 drawings, the students will do 40, and hand you the 10 best. I think this is unique.

KZ Obviously, the work ethic is a hugely positive thing, and I certainly learned that from my RISD education, but I do caution students about the equation of labor with value. I have seen a million students who buy into "The more marks I make, the better it is."

CH Likewise, I'm sure we have experienced in our teaching and professional lives that often there's no room to linger with something. Daniel, I like the lingering that happened when you had the students draw when they missed a week due to the hurricane. We think working hard means more lines or compulsively moving forward, but we somehow have to integrate lingering and boredom.

PP In a recent issue of *The Brooklyn Rail* [February 2013], the artist Mira Schor published a modest inspirational list of "productive anonymity," which included "the ability to experiment without much at stake except your own process of discovery…time to think and to *not* think; to look at art; to waste on dead-end art projects that no one will ever see again and that your best friends may remember better than you will…the ability to do things with just enough attention to make you feel like you are part of a world and can go forward, but not so much that your gesture becomes a trademark and a creative prison." I thought this was serendipitous.

SA Part of teaching is the transmission of curiosity and excitement in the search for one's voice in one's work. I share with students things that I have found and I also ask them to find something of their own. I sit beside them and we try to do this together. I do love engaging with students in that way. I sit at their desks, I face the same questions, and I know how much time it takes to produce something of value. So if I demand this of them, it's because I am demanding it of myself.

DL Here is the question I'm teaching: How do you create an ethics of making? From this standpoint, drawing is not about graphite on paper, it is about the development of the thinking inherent to making, the growth of a practice that will go on for many years.

Notes

My thanks to Laura Hoptman, Jean Fisher, and Stella Santacatterini—and their brilliant writing on drawing—for inspiring some of the thinking behind this conversation. Hoptman describes drawing as "what once was becoming" in her book *Drawing Now: Eight Propositions* (New York: The Museum of Modern Art, 2002), 12; Fisher and Santacatterini describe drawing as "thought only in the moment of making" in "On Drawing," in *Twice Drawn: Modern and Contemporary Drawings in Context*, Ian Berry and Jack Shear, eds. (New York: The Frances Young Tang Teaching Museum and Art Gallery at Skidmore College and Prestel Verlag, 2011), 169. "What once was becoming…thought only in the moment of making" could be the perfect description of drawing.

1. Fisher and Santacatterini, "On Drawing," 165.

2. Ibid.

3. Rosalind Krauss's iconic essay "Sculpture in an Expanded Field" (1979) analyzed a radical expansion of forms and concepts in sculpture in the late twentieth century.

Thingking

John Dunnigan

How does a RISD education promote critical making? John
Dunnigan, Professor and Department Head, Furniture Design,
introduces the practice of "thingking" as one path to developing
the creative process and understanding the symbiotic
relationship between thinking and making in art and design.
Drawing from the curriculum and connecting it to the work
of alumni, Dunnigan describes how thingking—the union
of critical making and critical thinking—supports a creative
process steeped in exploration and results in tangible outcomes
while promoting self-knowledge, self-expression, and an
understanding of one's relation to the world.

Recently I had a conversation with some of my students in which we tried to sort out what was happening as they developed their projects. We talked about what they were making, how they were making it, and why they were making it. We talked about how it looked. We talked about where it had come from, where it might go, and how their thinking was changing as they went through the process. At one point I asked them what we should call this process. Most of the terms we used seemed inadequate to describe it fully but one rang true: "thingking."

Artists and designers are form givers who bring ideas into the material world. In the studio we think about things. We think around things and through things. Yes, you could say we are engaged in thingking. Thingking expresses the symbiotic relationship between making and thinking in art and design, between object and idea. It connects critical making and critical thinking and relies on embodied knowledge, practice, and research. It integrates multiple ways of knowing and promotes holistic reflection and learning. Thingking is situated in contemporary and historical frames of reference. It includes the making of new artifacts that reflect the effects of the creative act on the maker, user, and system.

Thingking also involves engagement as it takes into account the consequences of those processes, phenomena, and artifacts. The presentation and critique of one's work is a key moment in the process of understanding what we really think. To stand beside an object that represents one's effort and growth and to get feedback on that performance can be a profound experience. This is often the point at which we compare what we thought we were doing with what actually happened, what discoveries were made along the way and what new doors opened. Though these artifacts may be idiosyncratic, they all tend to be material expressions of the complex interdependent relationships among culture, technology, and identity. We brought forth a thing and it shaped us as we shaped it. Thingking.

While thingking is contemporary, aspects of it have ancient underpinnings. When Pasiphae, the wife of King Minos of Crete, was charmed by

Fig. 18
Daedalus presenting
the cow to Pasiphae,
first century CE

the sea god Poseidon into falling in love with a bull, she turned to Daedalus, the most famously skilled person in the kingdom, to create a beautiful cow of wood so that she could climb inside and mate with the bull (see fig. 18). To make a lifelike cow out of wood implies expertise, internalized skills, familiarity with material properties, and the tools to manipulate them—all of which could be characterized as a kind of embodied knowledge.

The Greek myths predate Aristotle's fourth-century categorization of ways of knowing, which included knowing through skill (*techne*), knowing through intuition (*nous*), knowing through practical reasoning (*phronesis*), and knowing through fact and theory (*episteme*).[1] Mythology assumes integrated ways of knowing and demonstrates fluid relationships among them. The response to Pasiphae's request was dependent not only on physical skill and creativity. It also demonstrates that knowledge of materials and techniques, along with a deep understanding of structures and physiology, were necessary to make a faux cow that would protect a queen and support an amorous bull. The kinds of conceptual and intuitive capacities that were required to successfully complete such an extraordinary task incorporate other ways of knowing that span the realms of abstract and practical knowledge. This type of knowledge guides decisions about how tools should be applied to materials while helping to organize the possibilities of the whole endeavor, relying on critical thinking as much as intuition.

Embodied knowledge refers to skills and information that our bodies understand and remember as a result of sensory—especially haptic—experience and practice. Together, practice—here meaning repeated, thoughtful doing—and embodied knowledge help transform raw materials into a physical expression of an idea. Although the cultures of production and modes of training are very different today, embodied knowledge is still gained through haptic experience and sensory perception, particularly through working with one's hands. At first glance, this dynamic may be less evident in the field of design than other disciplines like painting, drawing, cooking, and making music, which rely more directly on physicality. For example, how much is a pinch of salt and how do you season to taste? How do the musician's fingers express the ideas and emotions behind the composition? How do you hold the brush or the chisel and learn to make a straight line or a crooked one depending on your intentions? This type of knowledge provides not only a way of expressing ourselves and communicating with others but also a way of knowing ourselves.

The human brain has not yet evolved into an organ that can understand fully without sensory perception. As Frank Wilson points out in his book *The Hand: How Its Use Shapes the Brain, Language and Human Culture*, any theory of human intelligence that does not acknowledge the interdependence of the brain and the hand is an impoverished one.[2] Artists and designers acquire embodied knowledge by doing and enhance their creativity by combining that knowledge with critical thinking. In practice-based disciplines, internalizing skills and building embodied knowledge increase opportunities for innovation.

Education in art and design is a nonlinear and open-ended creative process, integrating conceptual, intuitive, sensory, technical, and contextual components. At RISD, this happens through combining hands-on, intense, and immersive studio classes that integrate making and thinking with critiques that encourage reflection and redirection. Studies in the Liberal Arts enrich the experience by providing context and new perspectives. Woven together, these strands establish a theoretical and intellectual foundation for studio practice.

RISD's studio model is built around two key elements: *critical thinking*, the ability to process and evaluate information while challenging assumptions and employing multiple ways of knowing; and *critical making*, the process of creating things by altering materials and giving form to ideas. Critical making requires critical thinking and social consciousness along with embodied knowledge if it is to be distinguished from making in general. Critical making should also be understood as different than production where the thinking is complete before the fabrication begins. In critical making, the very process itself opens up new possibilities for deep, expansive thinking and the serious inquiry that stimulates discovery.

The Department of Furniture Design promotes thingking through one version of the RISD studio model. Students are encouraged to explore ideas and technique simultaneously, to integrate thinking and making, theory and practice. Undergraduates undertake a comprehensive curriculum, moving from focused and technically specific courses in the sophomore year to more experimental, research-based, and idiosyncratic practice in the junior and senior years. They develop embodied knowledge and haptic experience by beginning with hand tools and learning how to use them properly to shape and join wood, metal, plastic, textiles, stone, concrete, composites, and other materials not typically associated with furniture making. Technology is broadly defined and includes hand tools, machines, and digital tools. As a result, students might use a handsaw, a table saw, a laser cutter, a library, and a museum on any given project.[3] At the same time, they are guided through design principles and the process of conceptualization and design development via drawing and model-making, with all of these experiences culminating in the execution in real materials of their designs at full scale in three dimensions.

At both the undergraduate and graduate levels, courses have conceptual and technical challenges that align naturally in the studio environment, where intuition, abstract thought, and theory meet the material world. As our experience of the world becomes increasingly virtual and abstract, the experience of making physical objects and gaining multiple forms of knowledge in the process are increasingly valuable. Far from being anachronistic in a world where making is more and more digital, these types of knowledge are essential to the success of our alumni as they enter the professional world. Alumni of the Department of Furniture Design embrace developments in new technologies and many design things that often are made entirely, or in part, by others and by machines. But their experience with handling real materials and their capacity for taking a project from concept to finished "thing"—made possible by their immersion in critical making and thingking—are valuable personal and professional assets. These skills have helped to form the basis of many successful careers.

Indeed, while RISD Furniture Design alumni share a similar exposure to making, embodied knowledge, theory, and history, they use the practice of thingking in different ways. The raw materials, tools, and methods of production they choose are as different as the contexts and markets for their work. Two examples of alumni work, one individual, and one a partnership, demonstrate the value of broad pedagogic approaches and the multiple ways thingking is made manifest. These examples emerge from the same curriculum and learning environment, illustrating the adaptability of this form of education.

Matthias Pleissnig (BFA 2003 Furniture Design) demonstrated early on that he had a keen interest in form and sculpture. Throughout the sequence of courses and specific assignments, faculty guided him through the development of his own remarkable vision. His training in furniture design was useful in applying principles learned through hands-on making that helped to turn raw materials into the expression of complex ideas. In his current work, he uses 3-D modeling software to sketch compounding curves and then translates them into large-scale, one-of-a-kind objects made with wood that is steambent by hand, one piece at a time. Works such as *Providence* (fig. 19) explore the interaction of the human form with objects, but his exquisitely fabricated piece also celebrates making. Formally elegant objects may prioritize aesthetics over ergonomics, but they also suggest that the process of making is the thing against which all other considerations are measured. Matthias's work has been acquired by significant collections, and has been recognized with a Louis Comfort Tiffany Award (2009) and a USA Knight Fellowship (2010). His practice is very labor intensive, requiring a high level of expertise built on embodied knowledge as well as a deep understanding of his materials, their properties and potential, and ultimately, a physics of form in the way that process, material, and structure find embodiment in an idea.

The work of Theo Richardson, Charles Brill, and Alex Williams (all BFA 2006 Furniture Design) was diverse when they were undergraduates and included interests in scholarship, contemporary design, and installation/performance art, respectively. As partners in Rich Brilliant Willing (RBW), a lighting and furniture design manufacturer based in New York, they discovered the advantages of collaboration and openness as creative practitioners as well as the benefits of their department's diverse curriculum and culture of thingking. In their professional work, RBW highlights the use of pre-made components purchased from a variety of manufacturers to create unique products that are assembled in their workshop with simple tools and shipped directly to customers. Their making is technically, contextually, and ideologically different from Matthias Pleissnig's though they have the same educational background and a shared exposure to RISD's pedagogy. Even if their company brand seems to disassociate itself from the kind of production

Fig. 19
Matthias Pleissnig,
Providence, 2008

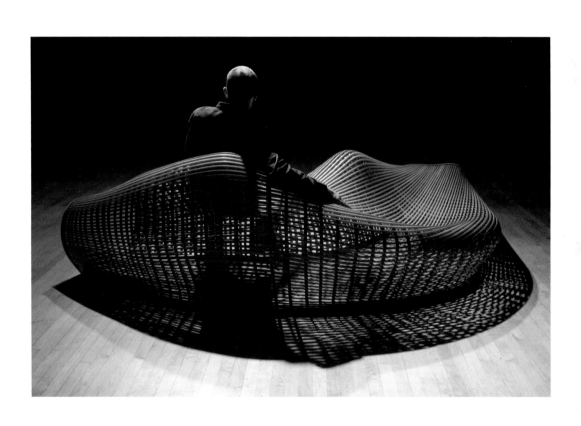

that requires craft expertise and embodied knowledge, to some extent, the aesthetic could only exist because of a deep understanding of how to make things. This is critical making that relies on multiple collaborative capabilities while consciously renouncing craft stereotypes.

The strength of RBW lies in their unique vision and in their capacity to reimagine and manipulate industrial components into poetic objects that raise the consciousness of their audience. Their products are disarmingly simple and potentially profound. *Bias Clock* and *Bright Side of Life* (figs. 20 and 21) are two stand-out product designs from 2010 that solve functional needs while encouraging users to think differently about time and light—projecting the embodied knowledge of making onto the user's experience of the objects. In short, RBW is a smart and timely business that celebrates the complexities inherent in the marriage of commerce, art, and design. Their partnership has received much critical acclaim in the last few years, including the ICFF Best New Designers Award in 2011 and *Forbes* magazine's "30 Under 30."

How does one department's curriculum encourage two such different yet successful approaches? Matthias's engineered, sensuous, and fluid forms help to redefine space, play with light and shadow, and relate to the human body, while RBW's work elevates found objects and industrial materials into thought-provoking products, bringing sophisticated simplicity to what could be purely utilitarian. The department is centered around the fundamental pursuit of giving form to ideas, with FORM (Furniture, Objects, Research, Materials) as a subtext. The curriculum has not forsaken making in favor of representation and a focus on systems and strategies, as have many design departments and institutions. Instead, the department fosters the exploration of a wide range of materials and approaches, and of conceptual thinking with hands-on making, which integrates human factors of furniture design with the social value of studio work and responsible citizenship.

At each stage of this pedagogical approach, the nonlinear nature of the design process encourages testing ideas through a variety of means, from drawing to deployment. Along that circuitous route, research plays a critical

Figs. 20 and 21
Rich Brilliant Willing,
Bias Clock, 2010;
Bright Side of Life,
2010

role in directing creativity toward innovation. There is a wide range of perspectives on what constitutes research in higher education, and how its definition varies across disciplines, particularly when comparing research in practice-based disciplines to research in the sciences and humanities.[4] Even subtler distinctions have been drawn between research in art and research in design. As an educator, I generally don't see an advantage to distinguishing between the two, but the differences are worth noting briefly. For example, artworks and art practice can constitute both the means and ends of research in art whereas design research is usually associated with problem solving. Generally speaking, research in practice-based disciplines like art and design means focused critical inquiry or sustained exploration aimed at discovery. This can take many forms, ranging from research into or through theory and philosophy, materials and processes, behavior and interaction, social responsibility and sustainability, markets and history, and, of course, form itself.

Research is an important developmental component in thingking, as shown in the work of Jamie Wolfond (BFA 2013 Furniture Design). When I asked Jamie to tell me about research in his new work, my favorite part of his reply was, "I wasn't failing fast enough." He was referring to his methodology, which includes a fairly rapid series of experiments characterized by a high level of spontaneity and a reliance on the empirical evidence of the results, all directed toward an outcome. By his own admission, he learns more from the failures than the successes and the process is open-ended.

The Furniture Design department's "Senior Studio" is focused on seating as well as the development of the proposal for their degree project, a capstone experience comprised of a related group of objects and a written component. In response to the five-week assignment to design seating using soft surfaces, Jamie came up with the idea of inflatables and sketched several versions of a stool with wood legs and an inflatable seat. He sought a manufacturer that could produce his design on an experimental basis and, in the process of discussions with them, made many adjustments to the form, learning about that technology and designing a product with potential for future production. When he realized that he might not get this stool completed by the critique deadline, he began to think about an inflatable object he could purchase locally and adapt to suit his intentions. Exercise balls fit the bill and he set out to bend and weld the steel wire frames himself that would alter the shape of the inflated balls, resulting in his *Ball Ottomans*. Several iterations and adjustments were made, each one having incremental improvements over the previous version, resulting in a group of finished pieces in time for the critique. During the critique, feedback provoked discussion about production at the broadest scale of making, what he could produce himself, and what he potentially could produce using outside fabricators when he had a longer time frame. The conversation influenced his approach to the subsequent project.

For the next assignment, which was to design a chair, Jamie decided to find some recycled materials that he could repurpose using the technologies available to him on campus. *Frumpy Chairs* (fig. 22) are the result of a remarkably prolific and intense investigation into reheating recycled low-density polyethylene thermoplastics into chair forms using sacks or bladders that Jamie cut, sewed, and stapled into rough, chair-like forms. The forms were filled up with ground-up thermoplastics then heated in an oven to a particular temperature (determined through lots of trial and error), at which point they were removed and draped over a steel form to make something that resembled a chair, once it cooled and became rigid. The chairs are hollow, which is the result of several tests to determine the ideal temperature and duration of the slumping to achieve the desired wall thickness. Although the process was messy, highly intuitive, open-ended, and maybe insufficiently documented, his was an empirical, focused, and directed inquiry that yielded original results. Jamie's work involves an idiosyncratic type of research that depends more on the fact that he is prolific and highly intuitive than it does on methodological consistency or scientific controls. It serves as one example of what research looks like in art and design education—and a case study in thingking.

While the undergraduate Furniture Design program has a core sequence of projects built around acquiring skills and expanding conceptual understanding in a progressive sequence, the graduate curriculum is highly experimental and individualized, as it attracts students from diverse backgrounds, each coming to RISD prepared in distinct ways for research in art and design. The graduate curriculum often begins with a challenge for new students to question what they already know and develop wholly new contexts for their work. This is effectively encouraged by specific assignments of different durations and subjects that encourage exploration of new materials and unfamiliar processes.

One outstanding example of the potential of this experience shows innovation through a specific focus on materials research. Daniel Michalik (MFA 2004 Furniture Design) entered RISD with a strong sense of contemporary design and very good woodworking skills. His response to the challenge of developing a new direction in his work was to explore underutilized materials and use them in new ways. When he discovered what he called the strange, unique, and useful qualities of cork, he was drawn to experiment with the material to see if he could make larger scale structural objects like furniture, an uncommon application. His 2004 thesis *Cork Stories* documents his research into cork's material properties, limits, and potentials. He studied its elasticity, porosity, buoyancy, impermeability, tensile strength, compression strength, and resistance to wear and discovered that it has a natural resistance to microbes and bacteria. He conducted a number of tests to see what was necessary to make parts of relatively large mass and how to create furniture-size objects with structural integrity.

Fig. 22
Jamie Wolfond,
Frumpy Chairs, 2012

This particular type of materials research considers aesthetics as much as material properties, which situates the inquiry and the product more in the realm of art and design than engineering. Daniel's *Cortiça Chaise Longue* (fig. 23), for example, utilizes cork's antimicrobial and buoyancy properties to function equally well on land or floating in a pool. His resulting body of work brought him wide critical acclaim and demonstrated good methodology for materials research in art and design. While Daniel developed this specific research into his thesis, the process of letting the material properties guide the design proved to be a way of working that was successful for him beyond the project, and he continues to work with cork and other materials, applying the same research principles.

While Jamie Wolfond's research derived from exploring how process can be the platform for thingking, and Daniel used the exploration of materials to generate new furniture forms featuring the properties inherent to those materials, work by Tanya Aguiñiga (MFA 2005 Furniture Design) illustrates another outcome of thingking. Her socially oriented furniture is as expressive of interpersonal relationships as it is of multiculturalism. *Hole Table* (fig. 24) may be an exercise in solving a problem that didn't really need to be solved, or it may be a humorous commentary on dining practices, but in either case it is an elegant object that serves to bring people together as tables do. What may be less evident is how it expresses Tanya's personal history. Tanya grew up in Tijuana and crossed the border into San Diego twice a day to attend school, spending hours each day in "the space between" of the border crossing. She carried the notion of "between" into the space between the top and bottom of the table, where dishes and flatware hover suspended in "the space between." The table is an experiment in approaching design from a behavioral perspective. *Zinacantan Chair* and *Teotitlan I* are similarly beautiful objects that invite us to see the potential of cultural diversity in the exquisite, unusual combinations of form and materials.

Tanya's use of modernist forms that look industrially produced is mitigated by soft and impermanent materials hand applied in several ways. The works resonate on aesthetic, technical, political, and commercial levels. In addition to furniture, Tanya's work includes jewelry, clothing, performance, and installation, often engaging multiple participants. The production of these works involves socially responsible practices and includes family and an expanding community of friends. The way things are made is important to her. For many years, Tanya has been a social activist and her commitment

Fig. 23
Daniel Michalik,
*Cortiça Chaise
Longue*, 2006

to community empowerment has been inseparable from the creation of art-works and products.

One of the most useful moments for creative development occurs in the middle of the fall term of a student's senior year, prompted by a require-ment to develop a written proposal for his or her degree project. Since draw-ing is often a more regular activity than writing for artists and designers, it is valuable for students to gain an understanding of the common ground between the two. For example, if drawing is essentially a way of represent-ing ideas, emotions, and things by inscribing marks on a surface, what happens if we look at writing similarly as communicating ideas, emotions, and things by inscribing symbols on a surface? Although they are vastly different in many ways, on some levels drawing and writing share some-thing fundamental: They are a means to develop ideas through the act of making marks and thus useful as comparative ways of expression and as integrated learning. Understanding the value of this type of learning, I have developed an exercise as part of an ad hoc seminar I call "The Loop of Thinking/Making/Drawing/Writing," in which we locate these four ways of doing on a circle with no clear beginning or end (see fig. 25, sketchbook of Sarah Pease, BFA 2013 Furniture Design). The point of this exercise is to demonstrate the value of circling through these ways of doing repeat-edly, where any of them might be the starting or end point of the process. This way of working unifies critical thinking and critical making and exemplifies thingking.

Timothy Liles's (BFA 2005 Furniture Design) senior Degree Project offers an excellent example of the power of this kind of integrated learning, and of how a deep understanding of the process of thinking and making can lead to influential and thought-provoking work. *The Wellness Project* investigated perceptions of health and proposed that for many people getting healthy takes a lot of work to achieve and, as a consequence, illness is the more normal state of being. With an effective undertone of humor, he designed pieces around three stages of illness awareness—prevention, detection, and medication.

Fig. 24
Tanya Aguiñiga,
Hole Table, 2005

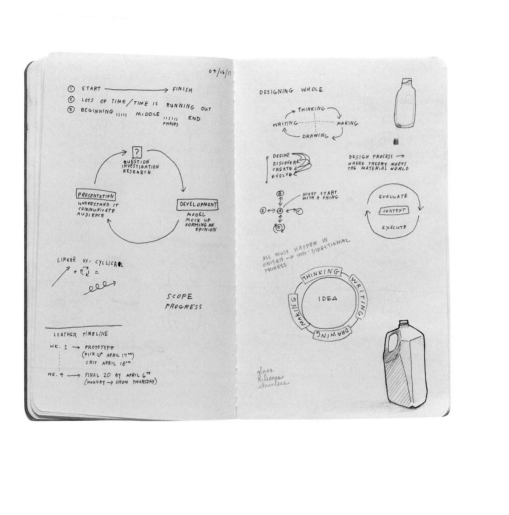

04/16/17

1. START ——————→ FINISH
2. LOTS OF TIME / TIME IS RUNNING OUT
3. BEGINNING ||||| MIDDLE ||||| END
   PHASES

?
QUESTION
INVESTIGATION
RESEARCH

PRESENTATION
UNDERSTAND IT
COMMUNICATE
AUDIENCE

DEVELOPMENT
MODEL
MOCK UP
FORMING AN
OPINION

LINEAR vs. CYCLICAL

↗ + 🐌 = ⟲⟲⟲→

SCOPE
PROGRESS

LEATHER TIMELINE

WK. 1 ——→ PROTOTYPE
          (PICK UP APRIL 17TH)
          CRIT APRIL 18TH

WK. 4 ——→ FINAL 2D BY APRIL 6TH
          (MONDAY → SHOW THURSDAY)

DESIGNING WHOLE

THINKING
WRITING ---- MAKING
DRAWING

DEFINE
DISCOVER
CREATE
EVOLVE

DESIGN PROCESS →
WHERE THEORY MEETS
THE MATERIAL WORLD

B
E ↔ A ↔ C   MUST START
   ↓   WITH A THING
   D

EVALUATE
CONTEXT
EXECUTE

ALL MUST HAPPEN IN
UNISON → NON-DIRECTIONAL
PROCESS

THINKING
WRITING
IDEA
DRAWING
MAKING

glass
philippa
stainless

The objects themselves are minimal wood structures, with paper, steel, and aluminum parts as required by their respective functions. Well Design, his temporary company established for the project, offered three products: a chair, a table, and a medicine cabinet. *Be Well Chair* (fig. 26) addressed sanitation phobia with a roll of paper across the backrest that could be pulled down the back and across the seat, then torn off and changed for each person who used it. *The Detection Table* supports self-diagnosis by providing a place for a small computer next to a sterile-looking aluminum clipboard. According to Tim, the clipboard had a contrived checklist for keeping records of past illnesses and sorting out symptoms while scouring the Internet for information on the latest maladies. *The Medication Cabinet* looked much like an archetypal medicine cabinet except that, in order to hold massive of amounts of medicines, it was long enough to reach from the top of the sink to the ceiling, and it came with a tall wood ladder. The furniture objects were the material expression of a contextually complete project and a holistic way of working that together formed a commentary on contemporary psychology and health care, and demonstrated the potential of furniture design to reflect and influence behavior.

Tim's work highlights the importance of directing art and design outward toward others. Tim has continued to do so in his professional career, which has included connecting regional artisans to high-end production work to support their economic viability. Such efforts remind us that no things are truly autonomous. Everything has a context. Although the critical making of things as a way of knowing and expressing oneself is perhaps the single most significant outcome of a practice-based education, that outcome would be largely inconsequential if it weren't directed toward human engagement. It is in relation to others that we come to know ourselves and see where art and design make a significant contribution to society—by raising consciousness, posing questions, solving problems, and providing new ways of understanding.

The thoughtful making of things creates new objects, but also new ways of thinking about manipulating materials and imagining complex forms,

about manufacturing processes and industry, about identity, behavior, and cultural commentary. Examples of RISD student and alumni work demonstrate how critical thinking and critical making support creative invention and expression, and suggest how engagement gives them greater purpose. They provide a glimpse into how an education that supports critical making through the development of embodied knowledge via practice and haptic experience, of critical thinking through context, research, and engagement, provides unique opportunities for innovation. In the twenty-first century, the fundamental pursuits of raising consciousness, solving problems, and creating new insights through original ways of seeing and making remain essential to art and design practice. Making things contributes positively to that. Critical making depends on critical thinking, and both guide the process of giving form to ideas, which can be observed and critiqued. Thingking is a practice that unifies critical making and critical thinking, and promotes engagement and reflexivity as part of open-ended exploration. Thingking is a practice that looks inward and outward and reflects on the effects of making on the maker, user, and system.

Notes

1. Aristotle, *The Nicomachean Ethics, Book VI*, in *The Basic Works of Aristotle*, Richard McKeon, ed. (New York: Random House, 1941), 13.

2. Frank R. Wilson, *The Hand: How Its Use Shapes the Brain, Language and Human Culture* (New York: Pantheon, 1998), 7.

3. The Fleet Library at RISD houses over 145,000 volumes, almost 400 periodicals, and a materials library. The RISD Museum contains 86,000 objects and a notable education department. Along with the Edna Lawrence Nature Lab, these make a remarkable contribution to the educational experience of students and faculty.

4. Among many current books on art and design research, see Henk Borgdorff, *The Conflict of the Faculties* (Leiden, Netherlands: Leiden University, 2012), 44–63. Though Borgdorff's emphasis is on artistic research, some of his observations could apply to design.

Fig. 26
Timothy Liles, *Be Well Chair*, 2005

Object Lessons

Sarah Ganz Blythe

How does the existing play into the creation of the new?
More specifically, what is the place of historical art and design
objects in the education of artists and designers? These
questions have been mainstays of art-school discourse for
centuries. Sarah Ganz Blythe, Director of Education at the
RISD Museum, revisits the long history of studying and
copying museum objects as a dominant form of art and design
learning and describes how RISD's faculty and students—
and the public—foster and form relationships with museum
objects that are expansive and multivalent.

For an artist or designer, to be in a museum is to be in the company of fore-fathers and matriarchs, idols and rivals. Within this context, objects can oper-ate as pedagogical models, or tools, that wrench open previously unknown life-worlds to cultivate competencies essential to artists and designers today. Indeed, works of art are the result of inquiry, experimentation, discovery, and innovation, and as such, they offer the opportunity to develop and exer-cise these very same skills. At the same time, it is easy to romanticize the connection between object and viewer and imagine that open lines of com-munication across time and place, between makers past and present, take form by simply situating artists in museums. While looking at and learn-ing from works of art has been essential to the creative process for centu-ries, how such generative relationships are formed is more complicated than that. Emerging artists and designers may not be innately equipped with the skills to decode and derive meaning from objects; such "cultural capital" is acquired through access, exposure, and instruction.[1]

Art of the past has long been the primary source and a pedagogical imper-ative in art and design education. The emulation of classical sculpture gave birth to art schools and museums in eighteenth-century Europe. Early paint-ings of museum interiors reveal artists stationed in front of masterpieces, copying the accomplishments of their forefathers. In representations of early academies, students may be seen drawing from nudes whose poses are informed by the classical sculptures that preside over the studio as mod-els of instruction. The masterpiece, literally a work of outstanding skill, was believed to hold the secrets of aesthetic virtuosity. Through the process of looking and remaking, such ideal forms could be internalized. This act of iter-ation called upon emerging artists to re-perform gestures, techniques, and processes to the extent that they could be surmised in a completed work of art. As such, the technical foundation essential to an artist in the classical tradition was established by reoccupying the place of artists past.[2]

Design education similarly recognized the importance of learning from historical models of expert craftsmanship. One of its most decisive moments emerged when London's Crystal Palace Exhibition of 1851 led to the eventual founding of the Victoria and Albert Museum, which would offer access to works of art to all and serve as inspiration to British manufacturers. The educational principle of the museum rested on the expectation that to see superior design would lead to the assimilation of good design standards, to the production of better design, and ultimately to improved industrial production. This built upon the academic model of emulation, but widened the scope beyond classical models to the material culture of the world. The display of objects in a museum for close observation and productive impact on industry became one of the driving forces behind the Rhode Island School of Design and a myriad of museums founded within schools and schools founded with museums in the later nineteenth century in Europe and the United States. The demise of this ideal was the undoing of many such relationships in the course of the twentieth century as the dismissal of established conventions prompted the modernist penchant for invention and innovation.[3]

Art and design education has long struggled to reconcile the foundational principles of academic training with the modernist trajectory that formed not to uphold but to oppose historical models. The infusion of critical theory into art schools in the mid- to late twentieth century further drew discourse away from historical objects, which appeared disconnected from contemporary studio practice and social issues. Despite these conditions, today's emerging artists and designers appear to find themselves in much the same way that students did in the Louvre more than 200 years ago—using objects as sites of research, investigation, and creation—in a museum temporarily turned studio. But the mastery of codified techniques is no longer the objective. Rather than make a precise replica through copying, students are asked to deeply consider technique, to investigate how the work is built, and then to *interpret* rather than remake the model. Take, for example, Painting faculty member Judith Glantzman's "Sophomore Painting I" assignment:

Select a painting in the Museum collection. Your selection can be an intuitive decision without an outside rationale. You are not required to "copy"
the selected work, but to interpret it. Try to understand the "bones" of
the painting, the interior logic, from the outside in. Look at its composition, color relationships, and formal and abstract aspects. Try to rebuild
the painting. Rebuilding the painting should lead to a deeper understanding of its many complexities—characteristics that are not evident on an
immediate, surface viewing—and to a deeper understanding of how to
build a painting of your own.

Printmaking faculty member Andrew Raftery described how an exercise
in close looking and analysis—"I ask them to notice the paper, ink layer, the
scale of the marks in relation to what is represented, the effects of time on
the work, and even to speculate on the appearance of the original matrix and
the chemical processing that may have been used to prepare the stone or
plate"—led to the unexpected: "Initially most students will attempt to force
the objects to fit into a pre-conceived idea. After engaging with the complexity of real things for a while, new compelling questions emerge."[4] In "Spatial
Dynamics II," Foundation faculty member Carol Lasch asks students to focus
on a single formal quality—volume—by looking at multiple objects:

Explore the properties of volume by creating an object with a structural
framework and a skin. The structural framework is an organizational
device that gives the piece form and creates order through the repetition
and rhythm of its components. The skin may be geometric and regular
or organic and sinuous. The skin can be pulled taut around the structural framework or loosely wrapped around it or contained within the
framework. However, the skin must allow the structure to be revealed
or expressed. Recall Victorian hoop skirts, the calash bonnet, Chinese
bridal headdresses, or other objects from the museum collection as varied expressions of structure and skin.

Undertaking assignments such as these, students turn objects into sites of formal research, investigation, and creation. Physical and durational engagement with primary sources supports the development of observational skills, deductive reasoning, and applied learning, embodying curator and educator Robert Storr's assertion that "making is thinking."[5] In an assignment for "Sophomore Drawing I," Painting faculty member Holly Hughes asks students not only to enter a dialogue in creating new works inspired by the collection, but to present the thinking process behind the making: "When you present the pieces for critique we should be able to trace your entire thought process—from the first encounter, through possible ideas and solutions considered, to the use of new visual language in your work."

Direct observation yields not only formal object lessons, but insight into process and context. Christopher Rose, faculty member in Furniture Design, asks students in "Graduate Furniture Design 2" to engage existing works of art as "points of departure," encouraging them to "notice what a work of art tells about its process of becoming," which might include "tactility, transformation, atmosphere, light, water, etc." or even be "connected to ideas in language; verbs, nouns, analogies, metaphors, etc." Thus, while objects in museums often appear finite and finished, the process of making can be made evident and evidence of the maker's hand extrapolated and engaged. Rose also encourages students to seek out contextual lessons in objects. In Charles and Ray Eames's leg splint—a molded plywood, lightweight, inexpensive, shock-absorbent splint designed for wounded World War II soldiers (fig. 27), he observes the "relationship between the development of ideas, how to make or manufacture objects, the appropriate techniques, what our value systems have to do with materials,...[and] responsible and intelligent use of materials in such a way that they achieve the objective, but with the lightest touch on the ecological systems of the planet."[6]

Museum objects, even ones from long ago, can also provide surprisingly contemporary insights into subject matter. Lee Johnson (MFA 2011 Ceramics) described an epiphany of sorts, provoked by a Greek amphora (fig. 28). "I had

Fig. 27
Charles and Ray Eames,
leg splint for U.S. Navy,
ca. 1943

GIFT OF DR. AND MRS. ARMAND
VERSACI, MUSEUM OF ART
RHODE ISLAND SCHOOL
OF DESIGN, PROVIDENCE

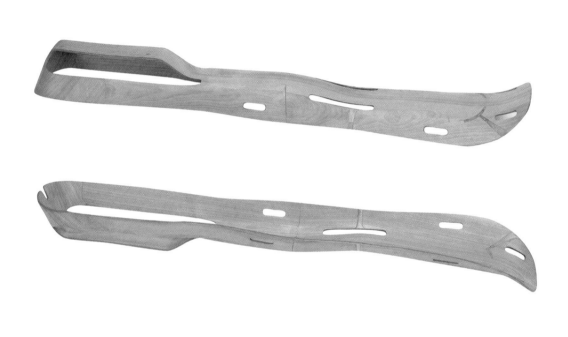

been agitatedly lost regarding how an object could relate to contemporary society and existence," he wrote. "Pondering the amphora it dawned on me that the figure [on its surface] depicted an idealized vision of Grecian society at the time.... I became aware of how we each cognitively build our own versions of existence.... Thus, a simple clay amphora, dating back to 500 BCE, gave me the means to explore how art objects have the possibility to relate to our multifaceted, fluxing existence. Or at least the existence we chose to portray."[7] A totally new body of work grew out of this unlikely and inventive line of thinking. Large, sinuous clay vessels recall the ancient example while their pierced, screen-like bodies and plugged-in handles evoke wired and digitally constructed identities. Lee's response is indeed a precise reflection of philosopher Giorgio Agamben's description of being contemporary as reading "history in unforeseen ways," "transforming it and putting it in relation with other times."[8]

Illustration faculty member Jean Blackburn describes a similar appreciation for finding contemporary relevance in the historical. A fragment of Egyptian furniture in the form of a bull's leg from around 2800 BCE (fig. 29), she observes, "immediately speaks to us. It's immediately recognizable as a piece of furniture precisely because we're still doing the same things with our furniture." At the same time, the fragment is unlike anything we would see today. "It's not a material we use any longer. It is aesthetically different from our tastes today." Blackburn finds tremendous significance in this temporal compare and contrast: "To understand that cultures can be simultaneously connected, have points in common, but also be very different, is an important lesson in dealing with our own globalized and multicultural world."[9] It is hard to imagine that digital images of such primary sources—available in bewildering abundance at our fingertips—could have had such an impact. These unbound and interpenetrating reproductions contrast starkly with the physicality of objects displayed in museum galleries. While the former is readily accessed and appropriated, the latter offers the "sensory experience of surviving historical events," as art historian Jules Prown suggests.[10]

Fig. 28
Greek, storage jar
(amphora) with
Apollo with lyre,
ca. 500–475 BCE

GIFT OF MRS. GUSTAV
RADEKE, MUSEUM OF ART
RHODE ISLAND SCHOOL
OF DESIGN, PROVIDENCE

Most works of art do not reveal extensive information at first glance. Instead they appear as puzzles, complex bodies of information that don't quite make sense. One way to start to derive meaning from what we see is to assign language to form, to name what is visually apparent, exercising observational skills. To describe is to begin to know. Interestingly, the act of describing can prompt related prior information, references, and personal experience into consciousness. In this way, deductions about possible meanings can take shape.[11] In their Foundation year, RISD undergraduates engage with this process when they write their first formal analysis paper in "History of Art and Visual Culture I." Here is faculty member Daniel Harkett's iteration of the assignment:

This assignment is designed to foster looking skills, develop your ability to link visual evidence to thematic discussion, and encourage you to express arguments clearly and concisely. Choose one of the following artworks: *Grave Marker*, 4th century BCE, Greek; or *Male Figure in the Guise of Hermes*, early 2nd century, Roman. Write a paper that addresses the following questions: How does form convey meaning in the artwork? How might your chosen work be connected to ideas and images you have encountered in course lectures, section discussions, and assigned readings? What effects do size, color, composition, and materials have on your perception of your chosen artwork? How is the human body represented in the work? How does the way it is represented contribute to the meaning of the work? Consider, for example, the treatment of skin, musculature, facial features; the presence or absence of clothing; the effects of pose and gesture. What does the maker of the work leave out and why? How might you characterize the relationship between the "real" and the "ideal" in the piece? How might form and function be related in your artwork?

Fig. 29
Egyptian, furniture
support in the
form of a bull's
leg, ca. 2800 BCE
HELEN M. DANFORTH
ACQUISITION FUND,
MUSEUM OF ART
RHODE ISLAND SCHOOL
OF DESIGN, PROVIDENCE

This shift from visual observation to deduction, from relative objectivity to subjectivity, underscores the fact that works of art rarely have finite meanings, but rather continually accumulate significance through interpretation. Progressive education has affirmed that such models are not simply received and accrued by the learner, but rather that the perceiver constructs meaning through experience. "For to perceive, a beholder must *create* his own experience," wrote John Dewey.[12]

Training in RISD's Textiles program emphasizes an objective and subjective working relationship with past models that leads to students expanding their notions of what is acceptable or possible in a field rooted in tradition. Textiles faculty member Anais Missakian's assignment for "Design for Printed Textiles" exemplifies the vast range of not only formal but historical and contextual information students glean from objects:

> Select a textile from the Museum. Study its historical context as well as its reoccurrence in later design periods, including the present day. Focus on a particular aspect or aspects of the chosen textile and start giving form to your own ideas by drawing, painting, and material studies. Using your historical reference as a starting point, develop a series of sketches, keeping in mind your application and end-use, and paying close attention to motif, scale, color, material, style, and technique. Resolve color, scale, mark, and shape as you clarify your ideas for your own collection of patterns, developing a contemporary point of view in your interpretation of the source.

Interpolating and experimenting across media, forms, and cultures, students in Missakian's course establish multilayered interpretations, both honoring and adapting their sources (fig. 30), as Arman Negahban's (BFA 2011 Textiles) own reflection suggests: "I tried to translate the color and construction of the woven Noh robe into a knit garment using rectangular shapes and theatrical bright colors. In keeping with Noh theater, the garment is meant to turn the wearer into a performer—bouncing, stretching, and changing color positions with movement."[13]

Fig. 30
Japanese, Noh theater
costume (*karaori*),
eighteenth century
GIFT OF MISS LUCY T. ALDRICH,
MUSEUM OF ART RHODE ISLAND
SCHOOL OF DESIGN, PROVIDENCE

RISD alumnus Spencer Finch (MFA 1989 Sculpture) has demonstrated the deep impact of this simultaneous play of homage and interpretation over a 25-year artistic practice. In the 1980s, when he was a student in Sculpture, Finch set up his easel in the RISD Museum in front of Claude Monet's *The Basin at Argenteuil* (fig. 31). Challenged by a classmate to copy the painting, he donned a beret and performed the age-old practice of replicating the accomplishments of his forefathers. At first he meant to be irreverent, finding the task irrelevant within the context of 1980s cultural politics and institutional critique. However, through the process of re-making, he came to understand the task Monet set himself and came to share in the artist's restless desire to give visible form to the invisible. Indeed, for the past two decades Finch has persistently pursued a study of light, color, and atmosphere through a variety of media—from delicate watercolor marks intended to capture the dust in a shaft of light to an immersive environment of hanging panes of glass that investigates light and reflection inspired by Monet's garden at Giverny (fig. 32). "I thought that Monet's work, especially the serial work, was about this idea of trying to capture something—a place, a moment, an impression, a light condition—and by repeatedly returning to it to get closer to its essence, while at the same time admitting the impossibility of doing so."[14] Thus, a historical work continued to act in the present and set the direction of Finch's work for decades.

In 2012, Finch returned to RISD to teach a studio that focused on negotiating artistic influence—a crucial aspect of his graduate experience—and to create an exhibition that consisted of his own work inspired by Monet's desire to "paint air." The exhibition, *Painting Air*, also featured a selection of works he curated from the museum's collection. Bringing an artist's perspective to curatorial practice, Finch created idiosyncratic sequences and unexpected juxtapositions, such as placing an ancient Peruvian textile (ca. 1200–1550) with open lattice beside the impulsive gestures of Willem de Kooning's *Black and White Abstraction* (ca. 1950). The selections reflected personal sources of inspiration and allowed the unconscious of museum

Fig. 31
Claude Monet, *The Basin at Argenteuil*, 1874
GIFT OF MRS. MURRAY S. DANFORTH, MUSEUM OF ART RHODE ISLAND SCHOOL OF DESIGN, PROVIDENCE

storage to "rear its head into the consciousness of the galleries."[15] Finch's curatorial foray has its roots in Andy Warhol's *Raid the Icebox I*—a seminal 1969 exhibition at the RISD Museum. Warhol scoured the RISD Museum's storage for his display, setting in motion the now ubiquitous practice of artist as curator "mining the museum."[16] His selection and arrangement of entire cabinets of shoes, Victorian umbrellas and Windsor chairs hung from the ceiling, and Native American blankets and European paintings reflected his personal tastes rather than master narratives, shuffling the deck of history and embodying novel ways of creating meaning.

Interventions into museum spaces such as Warhol's and Finch's are generally characterized as a form of "institutional critique." A method of artistic inquiry into art-world systems that emerged in the 1960s, institutional critique presents a way to readdress museum objects not as models for emulation, but as operatives that disclose and perpetuate the rhetoric of disciplines and the systemization of knowledge. Across time and media, the museum object becomes a co-conspirator as artists and designers develop working relationships with their medium. Artist interventions dispense with master narratives to offer novel ways of looking and alternative stories or propositions that highlight the ever-evolving meanings objects can assume. When an emerging artist or designer undermines institutional narratives by rewriting interpretations or inserting their work into codified museum displays, the museum becomes lab-like and studio-like—a space to test, play, and experiment with the formation of public discourse.

Brian Kernaghan, faculty member in Interior Architecture, offers a studio course—"The Narrative Museum"—devoted to this practice. His assignment "Six Objects in Search of a Narrative" (a play on Luigi Pirandello's "Six Characters in Search of an Author") exemplifies how RISD students are actively encouraged to rewrite and refresh established models:

> Identify six objects currently on display in any of the RISD Museum's
> permanent collection galleries that, placed together perhaps for the first

Fig. 32
Installation view
of *Painting Air:*
Spencer Finch, 2012
MUSEUM OF ART RHODE
ISLAND SCHOOL OF DESIGN,
PROVIDENCE

time, would be seen with fresh eyes. Thinking like a RISD Museum curator, juxtapose these objects to propose an interesting narrative idea. Come to class ready to articulate your connecting narrative. Include some basic information about each object and propose an exhibition title that expresses your narrative intention.

This open invitation to rethink interpretive strategies and construct new meanings can result in anything from the literal to the quixotic. For example, the Latin phrase *"omne trium perfectum"*—everything that comes in threes is perfect—leads a student to explore form and function in everyday objects made up of three different materials. The same assignment prompted another student to examine objects that incorporated the color blue, which revealed interconnectivity between cultures and across time—from Indian indigo dyes present in a Greek glass vessel from the first century CE through Bruce Nauman's use of blue neon tubes in the 1970s to the recent development of RGB LEDs, which allow Angela Bulloch to use light as medium (fig. 33). The invitation to think critically and poetically about the life histories and physical realities of objects offers deeply generative opportunities for students to negotiate and develop their relationship to art and design in the widest possible sense, while creating and communicating new forms of knowledge and engagement.

The museum offers all RISD students ongoing co-curricular opportunities to engage with its collections and spaces. "Work in Process" is an ongoing series of public talks in which RISD students discuss their own work in relation to selected objects in the galleries. Students are asked to "consider representing your artwork in various stages of completion, along with related tools and materials" and to "connect your work to the specific object(s) on view by addressing continuities and differences between the methods, materials, and processes of your work and the work on view." "Sitings," an annual competition, invites students to propose site-specific installations that "celebrate and exploit the RISD Museum—its architectural idiosyncracies,

Fig. 33
Angela Bulloch,
Copper 2, 2011
RICHARD BROWN BAKER
FUND FOR CONTEMPORARY
BRITISH ART, MUSEUM OF
ART RHODE ISLAND SCHOOL
OF DESIGN, PROVIDENCE,
© ANGELA BULLOCH

collection, and the habits of museum visitation." Winning projects receive a cash prize with implementation funds and the opportunity to work with museum staff throughout the exhibition process. These interventions might construct secret life-histories of objects through a pseudo-factual audio guide or question the conventions of museum architecture by inserting comically bent versions of classicizing columns into gallery interiors.

When students propose and realize an intervention that responds to the gallery context or the interpretations of its objects, they not only create in dialogue with the past or the conventions of display, their work enters a public dimension and shares an audience with the sites of their critique. Likewise, when emerging graphic designers investigate the museum, they not only develop crucial professional-practice skills, but test out operations in and against established systems of conveying information. Graphic Design faculty member Hans Van Dijk invites his students to cultivate deep public responses to the museum, as seen in his senior studio assignment "Dynamic Museum":

Using the possibilities of print media, exhibit design, and multimedia devices, develop a program and design prototypes allowing museum stakeholders to explore/experience works of art in the collection, contribute to, and disseminate information about the works of art. Through this project you will consider managing increased complexity in the scale of design challenges; allowing the people for whom we design to be participants in the design process; and understanding the importance of community. Select at least two thematic criteria that will facilitate a particular connection between the audience and the work of art: encountering works of art as a moving testimony to an era or idea; immersing the visitor deeply in the works' universe; encouraging visitors to think about their own relationship to the works; prompting personal associations and interpretations of the work; explaining the secrets of the objects; and rediscovering the work.

This design brief has led to diverse responses, from developing a communication and branding system designed to "to educate and inspire a passion for the arts and culture" to taking on crucial social issues such as "the lack of opportunities to culturally connect and educate the public about the arts."

Assignments and projects such as the examples here radically demonstrate that when emerging artists and designers share their perspective either verbally or visually with the public, they do more than situate their own practice within history. Sharing space with their artistic ancestors and their public, they recreate the museum as a dynamic reflection of the creative process and a generative site for questioning and dialogue. Through exploring objects as potent and multivalent sites, emerging artists and designers—and the public with which they engage—develop relationships to history that are physical, interconnected, and creative, facilitating the production of new meaning and forming "interpretive communities."[17] Thus, the museum as a whole expands and challenges notions of history and self. It permits an engagement with what philosopher Jürgen Habermas has called "the fantastic unbinding of cultures, forms of life, styles, and world perspectives that today no longer simply encounter each other, but mutually open up to one another, penetrate each other in the medium of mutual interpretation, mix with one another, enter into hybrid and creative relationships, and produce an overwhelming pluralism."[18]

This dynamic pluralist environment may fulfill RISD Museum Director Alexander Dorner's description, in 1938, of the museum of the future as a "power station, a producer of new energy."[19] While once the art school–museum was the civic center for altruistic cities and the generative hub of invention and innovation, today that model is exceedingly rare, yet exceptionally well suited to contemporary demands and potentials. If, as educator Carol Becker suggests, "what we mean by training artists...is imparting a commitment to the notion that being an artist means developing a creative approach to the complexity of the world," then the learning and making with and through art and design in museums and galleries presents the opportunity to develop the skills and disposition of mind to navigate such complexity.[20] Indeed, art schools with museums—especially where exchange between the two is responsive and rigorous—are uniquely positioned to operate as sites where not only artists but the public can learn about and make sense of the complexity of the world imaginatively. Museum collections provide the opportunity for *anyone* to develop generative and lifelong relationships with art and design. Through close looking, careful investigation, and thoughtful reflection, objects from varied cultures and contexts invite us to encounter complex social and cultural narratives, to draw upon personal knowledge and experience, and to imagine multivalent ideas and meanings—to let curiosity about the existing lead to the production of the new.

Notes

1. See Pierre Bourdieu, *The Field of Cultural Production* (New York: Columbia University Press, 1993).

2. For an expanded exploration of the pedagogical expectations for the role of historical objects in art and design education, see Sarah Ganz Blythe, "Keeping Good Company: Art Schools and Museums," in *Museums and Higher Education Working Together: Challenges and Opportunities*, Anne Boddington, Catherine Speight, and Jos Boys, eds. (London: Ashgate, 2013).

3. See Thierry de Duve, "When Form Has Become Attitude—And Beyond," in *The Artist and the Academy: Issues in Fine Art Education and the Wider Context*, Nicholas de Ville and Stephen Foster, eds. (Southampton, UK: John Hansard Gallery, 1994).

4. Andrew Raftery, "Curricular Connections: The College Art Museum as Site for Teaching and Learning," paper presented at College Art Association Conference, Dallas-Fort Worth, Texas, February 20–23, 2008.

5. Robert Storr, "Dear Colleague," in *Art School: Propositions for the 21st Century*, Steven Henry Madoff, ed. (Cambridge, MA: MIT Press, 2009), 64.

6. Interview with the author, November 14, 2011.

7. Lee Patrick Johnson, *The Cultural Apocalypse*, Master's Thesis, Rhode Island School of Design, 2011.

8. Giorgio Agamben, "What Is the Contemporary?," in *What Is an Apparatus? and Other Essays*, trans. David Kishik and Stefan Pedatella (Stanford, CA: Stanford University Press, 2009), 53–54.

9. Interview with the author, June 18, 2012.

10. Jules Prown, "Mind in Matter: An Introduction to Material Culture Theory and Method," *Winterthur Portfolio* (Spring 1982): 3.

11. This framework is informed by Jules Prown's approach to interpreting material culture, in "Mind in Matter."

12. John Dewey, *Art as Experience* (New York: Penguin, 1934), 56.

13. RISD Museum, *Exhibition Notes*, no. 37 (Summer 2010): 4.

14. Spencer Finch in conversation with Judith Tannenbaum, *Exhibition Notes*, no. 39 (Winter 2012): 3.

15. Ibid., 6.

16. See *Raid the Icebox 1 with Andy Warhol: An Exhibition Selected from Storage Vaults of the Museum of Art, Rhode Island School of Design* (Providence, RI: Rhode Island School of Design, 1969).

17. See Stanley Fish, *Is There a Text in This Class? The Authority of the Interpretive Community* (Cambridge, MA: Harvard University Press, 1982).

18. Michael Haller, *The Past as Future: Jürgen Habermas interviewed by Michael Haller*, ed. and trans. Max Pensky (Lincoln: University of Nebraska Press, 1994), 119.

19. Alexander Dorner, *The Way Beyond "Art,"* 2nd ed. (New York: New York University Press, 1958), 147.

20. Carol Becker, "The Artist as Public Intellectual," in *Review of Education, Pedagogy, and Cultural Studies* 17, no. 4 (1995): 387.

Conversation: Materials

Kelly Dobson

How does our relationship with materials shape both our
art-making practices and our ways of experiencing the world?
Kelly Dobson, Associate Professor and Department Head,
Digital + Media, asked Anais Missakian, Professor and
Department Head, Textiles; Jocelyne Prince, Assistant
Professor, Glass; Eric Anderson, Assistant Professor, History
of Art and Visual Culture; and Mark Pompelia, Visual + Material
Resource Librarian, Fleet Library at RISD, to speak about
the unique ways in which they interact with their materials—
whether fiber, glass, text, or archive. The conversations often
returned to the idea that the artist/material relationship
is itself a dialogue, in which both the artist and the material
participate, listen to one another, and evolve together.

And there must be simple substances, since there are composites; for the composite is nothing more than a collection, or aggregate, of simples.... And since every present state of a simple substance is a natural consequence of its preceding state, the present is pregnant with the future.
—Gottfried Leibniz[1]

In the past decade, resource books on materials for artists and designers have offered a foray into the available materials for use in practice as well as the materials currently in research and development stages.[2] These books mainly focus on telling stories about materials, with materials being, in general, a range of resources for human use. They are incredibly useful as field guides and I often refer my students to them. The point of this series of conversations is different. It shares intimate frames of encounters with materials and with the potentials of materials.

In contemporary Western culture, we tend to think of most material as a passive substance. We try to work with materials as if we are the only ones leading, as if we have all the control and creative contribution in the collaboration. Occasionally we think of materials as tools—sandpaper used to alter a surface, water and garnet used to water-jet cut, scrap metal and wood used as wedges and prying agents—but we are rarely invited to think about materials as the agents of action, as forceful substances with tendencies, perhaps even desires. Once we recognize these properties and learn to work with them, we become sensitive to their potency and possibility. We realize that materials often lead. This is a vital part of what we teach and learn at RISD.

Artists and designers train to approach the lively aspects of the materials with which they work with multileveled engagement and creative play. They become absorbed in the conversations, dip in and out, and enter experiences of making collaboratively in working states that reject the question, "Where does your input end and the input of the material begin?" Most people experience this in one way or another daily. People are material, too, after all; our materiality renders us in the mix.

Materials and forces are the basis of making. We apply pressure and imagination to materials and they become meaningful to us. Energy and velocity become meaningful when used in relation to materials. Materials touch. We push on them and they push us. We remember that intelligence is not just about information. It is not at all just in the head. There is intelligence in the body and in movement. In the moments when artists and designers take cues from their materials, they find themselves engrossed in this communal space. It is not about commanding material as if in a one-way relationship. Control is too fallible an assertion. Material is not passive, brute, inert, or dumb. Material has potential and activity independent of what we may see in it, make of it, or do with it. Material is as much force and energy as it is matter and volume. Materials that you think you drive could drive you. Or, you can take turns.

Anais Missakian, Professor and Department Head, Textiles

KD How do you engage with your materials?

AM Probably more than other materials, fiber—or cloth, what fiber can be made into—is connected to the human experience; cloth holds history, culture, memory, emotion, comfort, and protection. Yes, buildings surround you, but fabric actually touches you. Fiber is one of the most interesting elements to study in order to understand culture, society, and practice—death practices, customs, and religious traditions. Much of a story is told through fiber—be it cloth that is very rustic, basic, or fundamental, for example, or a particular fiber that is extremely rare.

KD Such as a cotton garment versus a spider-silk robe.

AM Exactly.

KD Do fibers and textiles hold memory and history on different levels? On the fiber level with the sheep, the plant, and the farmer; on the textile level as it is made; and then again on the level of the textile as it relates to cultural practices?

AM Right, but then fibers and textiles hold history on still another level. Weave structure contributes to performance and durability, but it also contributes to beauty and aesthetics. We can date and place cloth by its technique and materials. For instance, a cloth that has been block printed, screen printed, or digitally printed is located in its time. Yet textiles are not only defined by technique, performance, and function. Our greater contribution to textile making is as artists and designers.

KD It contributes to the cloth's function when someone sees it and has an experience, and that counts.

AM It does count, or we wouldn't be doing it. But what is aesthetics? How does it add to our experience? What one wants to think about in making textiles for interior spaces is, "Am I making beautiful things that make life more pleasant, or are my decisions in structure, color, and pattern really going to affect how someone lives?"

KD How would those decisions affect the way someone lives?

AM They could affect one's ability to be contemplative or ability to slow down, for example. If you walk into a space that is dominated by an optical pattern, you are going to act uniquely in that space. You might move through that space faster. You might not be able to sit in it. Let's say you want to make a contemplative space, you could achieve that visually, through color, scale, and quality of mark and shape, or you could do it through having some sort of ...

KD ...soft felt, or sound-absorbent material.

AM Yes, so there is a great ability to manipulate an environment in that way. For clothing—going beyond the performative or the functional—we make visual choices. The patterns, colors, and materials I wear are a reflection of who I am. Why is one person drawn to a dry, rugged fabric while another person is more attracted to a very beautiful silk? What one is naturally drawn to is fundamental.

KD To wear? To look at?

AM To whatever. It's what moves us. The haptic is so important. You can't look at a textile without wanting to touch it. The impulse to touch cloth is so basic; it's readily malleable and changes in your hand. Fiber material isn't the end in itself; it is only through the making that it forms into something that might be the end. So, it is what happens on a piece of furniture, on the body, in space; cloth is not the end, it has to be formed into something.

KD It is immediately malleable and at the same time contains and carries so much of its experience and the experience put into it in process.

AM Yes. And this is as important for the future as it is for the past and the present. As we work toward the future, what we recognize through fiber or cloth is going to be very interesting.

KD Will the new, synthetic fibers have this kind of memory?

AM Right. Or, if they do, will it be fundamentally different? Will it be as emotional, or as expressive, or carry as much information about culture?

KD What will the new fibers do, culturally?

AM The performative aspect of new fibers is very advanced. It is often the actual fiber properties that make a cloth stronger, softer, more brittle, able to withstand extreme temperatures, baffle sound, or wick water. It has been this way from the early days: the use of fur and wool to keep a house or a body warm, for example. New developments in fibers go after those same fundamental aspects of function and performance.

KD Considering these new fibers, are there some examples that you are especially drawn to?

AM Thinking of high function, certainly man-made spider silk for its strength. Para-aramid synthetic fibers are no longer new, but stand out for their protective qualities. These are very expensive fibers developed through years of research.

KD Spider silk looks like gold. Have you seen it?

AM Yes, it's incredible. But my question about innovations such as these is always, what is our role, as designers and artists? How do we work with these materials differently than would an engineer? Most material development in the modern world has been for organizations like the military or NASA. I think this is because they demonstrate a real need. The question of what is needed, for existence, in the desert or in space, drives innovation. So what drives origination when you don't have those needs is a really important question.

KD As artists and designers working with materials and/or inventing them, are there sets of needs we can identify as urgent? How do we take an artistic approach to the question of what humans need?

AM We can make great contributions in identifying urgent needs. Fine arts contribute to advancing culture and society and are as important to human need as a particular design solution connected to a particular function and use. Design should be infused with both the tangible and intangible.

KD This probably happens in the abstract, on a longer time scale, so we are not used to considering these less tangible needs as incredibly urgent.

AM Right. Because we don't need them in the moment.

KD Or we don't know we need them.

AM You're right—that value is not always recognized in the present.

KD I believe that ideas emerge out of the making. Yes, you can start with an idea, but it is in the messing around, that kind of deep immersion into the making and touching of the material, that ideas really develop.

AM The ideas emerge from the making. Allowing a dialogue with the fabric, the fiber, or the yarn is how the ideas become more fully formed. My teaching emphasizes the importance of the iterative process. One starts with an idea but that idea is not set as the end, but rather a beginning. It is through playing with the materials that you truly come up with something new.

KD And you go in with an openness, ready to listen to what the materials are saying back to you. And through material exploration there is a redefining of technique, also. Your current student, Agustina Bello Decurnex [MFA 2013 Textiles], calls one of her material inventions "knit printing"—she's thinking about how a print can become a three-dimensional structure (fig. 34).

AM Right. Agustina's work is a great example. Agustina samples tirelessly, creating a myriad of exciting possibilities. In contrast, if a student isn't making enough, the ideas don't have the chance to develop depth.

KD How do you guide students into the process of getting their hands into the materials, which then defines what the ideas and the materials become?

AM This is a really basic example. A student makes this unbelievably beautiful folded paper construction. Then he or she wants to interpret that in fabric, or through fiber construction. It's not possible, because paper does its own thing. So, it's about honoring the material and not trying to make it do something that it inherently doesn't want to do. It's about saying, "The material has control here," rather than, "I am going to control the material." Every material has its own set of things that it wants to do. So, you go back to the student and say, "Don't start with paper. Start with a material that you think is going to fold absolutely beautifully and do the thing that you are looking for functionally." And right away the material then starts to define something wholly different from what the paper would, and that in itself is profound. Every material has its inherent properties that through creative investigation can find its richest form.

Fig. 34
Agustina Bello Decurnex,
To the Sea, 2012

Jocelyne Prince, Assistant Professor, Glass

KD Is there ever a blurring between you and your materials, in which it is not really easy to know who is doing what?

JP Yes, and I think the emphasis on experimentation is one of the really interesting things about RISD, because it really is about that dialogue between you and the material, you and the idea, and you and the process. You set up conditions in which you are making the choice of what you are testing or experimenting with, but it is in anticipation of a response from the material, and it is your responsibility to observe the response and then reflect on it. To think, "What is that? What does that mean? If I do this thing, how do I actually make that part of the meaning of the piece, part of the process that I'm working with, part of the conditions of these actions?"

KD How do you communicate with and work together with your materials?

JP A lot of what we do in glass, as opposed to thinking about skill and mastery, is think about dialoguing with materials in terms of their properties. "Properties" could be synonymous with "agency"—what agency does the material have? How does it end up being part of the political or social implications of an object or action? A lot of RISD departments that deal very heavily with material are not limited by expectations. What is produced is not even necessarily an object. To aim for an end object creates a narrow view of what is possible. It is much more exciting to think, "If a material can have a vocabulary, what vocabulary can it have?"

KD Do you mean, if the material articulates, what does it say and do?

JP Yes. As an example, if you take glass and grind it up, atomize it, and then reconfigure it together, that process alone gives it meaning. Glass is a material that we make; it is not a material that is found in the world. You can't turn it back into sand, though you can grind it up, melt it together, and it looks different and has different physical properties. Those physical stages are part of the vocabulary of a piece and of the materials. Industrial glass, studio glass, blown glass, lampwork glass, and scientific glass—each has its own vocabulary. In one process you take a preformed tube and expose it to a flame—if you are sensitive to the material and its properties, then you are working within its specific vocabulary. You could choose to completely ignore that vocabulary and just create a certain object. Or, you could actually listen to it and work together as a kind of collaboration.

KD Does the vocabulary of working with glass translate to people who are not engaged in this process?

JP A potential problem with the glass world is this idea that it stands outside of other things, when it doesn't. Glass is a material that is "in between": it's a transparent, invisible material in which information can be revealed only through light. That is meaningful to a broader audience than just specialists. Yes, you can become a specialist in glass, but it is uninteresting if that doesn't have anything to do with the rest of the world. I think it is our job as specialists to think about that rather than, more traditionally, to think about how to make a perfect goblet. It's a similar conversation to that of beauty in terms of painting. What is a perfect object? What is a perfectly blown glass object? That has less meaning than, What is this material? And what can it do?

The question, "What is the perfect object?," on the one hand, is very antiquated, while on the other hand, "What is material?" really addresses some of the newest technology. I was just looking at Corning Willow Glass, this new, ultrathin, flexible glass, with which they want to make digital apparatuses that are actually body forming. For instance, a smart phone that you can wear on your wrist that is actually bendable glass.

KD What might it mean, in terms of being a person, when we are wearing conformable membrane machines as prostheses, influencing our senses and possibilities?

JP I think it invites us to ask a lot of really interesting social questions. What is an interface that is not even an optic anymore, that is connected to your body? It would be great to engage these really out-there concepts and to see people grappling with their pragmatics.

KD I remember first cutting and grinding glass in the studio with you.

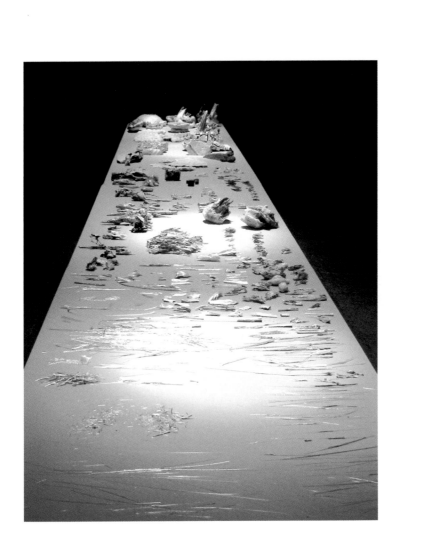

JP Yes. It makes me think about a former student, Anjali Srinivasan (MFA 2007 Glass) who took glass, ground it, and began mixing it with flour, in an almost mimetic experiment. As in, "This material looks like this material. Okay, why are they different?" A simple thought—not simplistic, but direct. So she mixed glass dust and flour together and got this material that she called "puffy glass" (fig. 35). It was technically glass, but it was the weight of Styrofoam.

KD So she kiln-baked the mixture and the flour burned out?

JP Yes, she "cooked" it with the flour in a domestic process, in a sense, like making bread. And because she was using flour, she saw the possibility of growing molds on it. It posed all these other conditions, the viability of a glass that can grow material and be part of another kind of dialogue. But then she had to ask, "What does this material mean?"

KD That is really interesting.

JP We look at glass as a natural material. That is part of its properties. We know glass is a man-made phenomenon, but there actually are natural conditions that create it. You know, all of a sudden, a volcano! Extreme heat, a certain amount of sand, and you get obsidian. You add too much rock to it and it's not glass anymore, it's pumice. We had a student looking at obsidian, and he posed the question, "Can I melt it?" That would require a temperature much higher than we can get, but the process is not about coming to a stop like that. Instead, we put it under the simple condition of being exposed to the heat of a glory hole furnace and it did this amazing thing. The gases that were trapped inside released. We couldn't bring it to a liquid state, but it became very airy and light. He figured out parameters using very old technologies—how to cut and grind glass, but also how to heat it. So he was using all these traditional ideas to form obsidian in a totally nontraditional way to make nontraditional things. That sets up a whole new vocabulary.

Fig. 35
Anjali Srinivasan,
999 Fragments of
Puffy Glass, 2007

KD You make an action and the glass responds back, and while that response isn't a word, it is reciprocal, and it is a dialogue.

JP It is a reciprocal dialogue that uses a specific vocabulary.

KD I'm very excited by what you're saying. Watching glass artists at work, it is easy to observe, from the outside, a dialogue in terms of balancing moving molten masses of glass and multiple human and non-human bodies, collaborating in the different roles necessary to blow glass. But what is so fascinating about this other dialogue that you are describing is that it is on a different time scale than that which we can, from the outside, readily observe. There are ideas that suddenly become present, and there are questions that may emerge that one may mull over for days or weeks before responding. Much of this may not even be conscious. The thinking is not directed. As you say, we don't set out to make a known object. Likewise, we don't work knowing what our questions and responses will be until they unfold in a reciprocal dialogue. It reminds me of your student who was making glass on the beach by attracting lightning.

JP Yes, those kinds of things are amazing—the setting up of conditions that take on or recreate natural processes within an industrial process. The implications of what it might mean—is it optic or action?—is exciting and I think it has everything to do with this moment.

KD Something happens—experiential, physical—and something happens back. And that is not a quantifiable thing, but it's very meaningful.

JP Yes, and if you think about virtuosity or a certain kind of skill, that is something one can quantify, but it can have absolutely no meaning. You can do "X" with some glass, but you haven't asked any questions, so you really don't know anything. It is a little bit of a struggle because you have to have both. The RISD approach is to understand some of those traditional skills, and in some sense strive for them, but then to question them simultaneously, and challenge them. And that's when it gets really interesting.

Eric Anderson, Assistant Professor, History of Art and Visual Culture

KD As an art historian, how do you interact with materials?

EA I study materials in the way designers work with materials, but I also have my own materials. One set of materials is the documents that I use to extract ideas for understanding and teaching history. Those fall into several categories. Books and art historical literature put me in conversations with other art historians who are thinking about similar historical material. And there are old books that represent voices and ideas from the past that were circulating around particular objects. There is something very physical about working with an old book. For instance, my research right now is on nineteenth-century ideas about the interior. A great resource for this has been period publications about interior decorating that were for the consumer, the homeowner (fig. 36). These are old books and magazines that people had in their homes or that designers looked to for advice about decorating. In that case, the physical object is really important.

KD That idea of the physical object putting you into conversation with another time is so interesting. Can you say more about how that works? Do you talk back?

EA There are certainly physical ways that I interact with books. I make all kinds of marginal notes in books. I'm always assigning my students to read from the same books I'm reading. When that happens, I have to erase my notes, make a clean scan so that they can make their own notes, and then I go back and re-read and take new notes again.

KD I do that too!

EA I like to get students to see books as an active material that they can have an ongoing dialogue with. The tendency is to think, "Here's my reading assignment, I'm going to read it. Okay, it's in my head now, toss the book, come to class, I'm ready to have a conversation." But I always bring the

THE JAPANESE PARLOR.

The second drawing-room communicating on the south wall the first one, is known as the Japanese Parlor. Here all the furniture and decorations are in Japanese taste, and so far as they be of Japanese origin. The very thick upon the wall is a slavophive imitation of some masterpiece of Japan art, with a graceful line all surrounded with choicest crystals in which the Roman majestic for the hours enough to be understood through that running tracery of the Mongolian alphabet.

A peculiarity which especially imposes on the eye in the ceiling; it is so insistantly Eastern in character that the young visitor, closing then the room with eyes distinctively fixed, is persuaded that the genie has transported him if not into a bower of Aladdin's palace in Cathay, at least into the confines of a favorite princess in the Japanese mandarin. Through the same silent, of its open transverseing of translucent bambo, appear

the angles of a bijwood of bamboo, lined and inlaided complete with the golden tints of that beautiful wood. The effect is not only gentle novel and known, but completely graceful. Not only is the trellis of tabouroret, minutereth moresgilse Japanese-looking, with its waving, deceptively imitative of the real Minca or Sunbio lacquer, physical books that we've read into the classroom so that they are part of the conversation. If a student is saying, "This idea from the reading is really important," I can say, "Give us a page number, let's all put our finger on it and read it together and then digest it from there." That way we are interacting with something physical. Thinking evolves and becomes much more concrete through that kind of back and forth. You read. You come up with an understanding of what you've read. And then you verbalize it with other people, and they verbalize something back to you. At that point, if you go back to the original concrete object that you are working with, the text, and read it again, you get something new and you reverbalize it and there is that potential for an ongoing back and forth. When I assign papers, my assignments always emphasize going back to the documents that we've been working with. My hope is that when students write their papers they will return to this process of going back to the physical text, reading it, processing it, writing something, going back to it again, reading it, writing something, and processing it.

KD So, if you have not posed a question or experiment to your material, listened back, and had a dialogue, you really have not learned anything.

EA Posing questions to the text is absolutely critical. I often pose to students an initial question before they read a given text. Then, when we start the conversation after they've read, I first get the students to fire out some key terms that they see as being important to the text. I get those up on the board and then we go back to the text and pick out these terms, and say, "Frank Lloyd Wright is talking about 'materials' here. What do materials mean to him?" We have to specify what arguments are being made, for example, "Frank Lloyd Wright is talking about materials here and he means 'A,' then at the end of the text he brings the term back and means 'B.'" We identify a category and pose questions about that category.

KD Does this push and pull also happen on the level of the words, on the level of language, as material itself?

EA Yes, absolutely. Part of what I want to do for the students is model that process of talking around and through an object and a question, and verbalizing it in different ways so that meaning becomes clearer. The process of starting with a key term and working outward from there is also part of trying to find the right language. When we come up with a list of 20 terms, we find that a lot of these terms are very closely related; if we can start to cluster them, we come up with more complex ways of verbalizing their meanings in relation to the text.

KD It can bring students past the anxiety of verbalizing an idea, and then going from there.

EA Anybody can throw a word at you. Then you can push it and say, "You identified the term 'process'—can you point to a passage in the text or can you say something more about it?" Using a system that builds from fundamental blocks upward to greater complexity helps open up the conversation and also helps the students create a structure for thinking, proposing paper ideas, and composing their ideas.

KD The materials of language and ideas behave on an atomic level, but also form larger ideas and communicate with each other and the students, resulting in larger assemblage behaviors.

EA Yes, with materials, you start with one material and combine it with another material and it works differently once it is combined.

KD What other materials do you work with, besides books and texts?

EA I go to the RISD Museum and I look at artifacts. Then I come back into the classroom and I show students images of the artifacts. Or I go out on the street and I look at buildings, and I come back and show images of buildings. The way that the physical artifact relates to the reproduction is another interesting question that historians deal with. What we can get out of an image of Marcel Breuer's tubular steel furniture versus what we get out of going to the museum and seeing it versus if we are able to pick it up and turn it around in our hands. For an upcoming course, with John Dunnigan in the Furniture Design department, we are working out a plan to go into the museum with our students and talk about some chairs and pick some objects that demonstrate a process of working with materials and a manufacturing process in really interesting, visual ways. We will look at Harry Bertoia's wire chairs, or the tubular steel furniture from the 1920s that Breuer and Mies van der Rohe and others were making. And the '60s plastics are so fascinating, for example, Verner Panton's cantilevered plastic Stacking Side Chair (1959–1960). You can learn something about the materiality of the object, about the actual physical properties of tubular steel or injection-molded plastic, which is not nearly as clear from seeing a reproduction.

KD Do you think it would be important to sit in the chair?

EA Yes. I went to the Furniture Design department critiques last semester and everybody was sitting in the chairs and bouncing around, sensing how the parts work together, and how the structures behave. In the reproduction, we tend to think about a chair as a kind of autonomous sculptural object, unless it is an image that is somehow staged to demonstrate its use.

KD Images have a way of transforming the meaning of an object, by staging it in some way?

EA Yes. For instance, I use an image of Breuer's *Wassily Chair* (1926) all the time. This chair represents Breuer as an architect and designer confronting and recognizing the possibilities of a material—bent tubular steel—that hadn't been used to make domestic furniture. He had found it in bicycles, and he thought, "This has an application for furniture." He thought about how the inherent properties of tubular steel, when it is bent by machine, can be visualized and used to come up with a fundamentally new form for the chair. He started with this continuous tube that created the legs, arms, and back. This initial chair had six or eight different pieces of steel joined together, but then he gradually refined this to the point where he used one singular tube that formed the back, seat, base, and the leg in one single, cantilevered form. Then when it is staged for this photograph, featuring a woman in a mask and modern dress, it is completely transformed, or at least adds new layers of meaning.

KD The chair is one kind of material artifact and the image is another kind of material artifact, both with very different meanings. And both are materials you engage in dialogue with.

EA Yes, and the dialogue extends to include books, texts, words, images, objects, and physical artifacts.

Mark Pompelia, Visual + Material Resource Librarian,
Fleet Library at RISD

KD The Graham Visual + Material Resource Center at the Fleet Library just opened last year—how did it come to be?

MP There had been the idea for this resource center at RISD for at least a decade or so. Materials are central to the work of most departments, but there was not yet a central space for material resources to come together. When the library building was renovated, what is now the Graham Visual + Material Resource Center (or MRC) at that time housed a slide collection. By 2005, slides were no longer seen as a twenty-first-century medium, so there was a sense that the slides would not need this space much longer and that a material collection could be housed here. In 2012, we received a Champlin Foundation grant that largely funded the renovation of this space. The MRC now includes around 20,000 objects in a central setting, open to the entire campus and to the public, as opposed to smaller, separate collections that would be housed in individual departments.

KD Can you talk about your experience in the MRC so far?

MP Since the beginning, we have been assembling a critical mass of materials. In the second year, we renovated the space to encourage and facilitate faculty and students' material inquiries. As we continue bringing in new materials, we are working on developing a taxonomy and database.

KD What meaning and connections emerge between people and materials?

MP The world of material knowledge is changing so rapidly. Materials are becoming known and accessible at an increasing rate and in ways that are unpredictable. The thing that makes this collection exciting is not just that it is big and beautiful but that it is available campuswide. A student from the Textiles department will see these objects differently than students from the Furniture Design, Jewelry + Metalsmithing, or Landscape Architecture departments. And so we have the potential for pollination across disciplines.

KD Cross-pollination in the sense that students will come here from all disciplines, but also in that they may then respond to their experience and make a new material, or materials, which they will in turn bring back to you?

MP Yes. In fact, a graduate student who works with us received a RISD Academic Commons Program grant to curate an exhibition of student-made, rather than commercially made, materials (fig. 37).

KD What are students typically looking for when they come to the MRC— particular materials, or...?

MP Right now we are still organizing the collection by composition, which is a sort of traditional approach. It reads from left to right as metals, woods, glass, mineral, animal, plastics, polymers, and composites. However, half of the time people come in not looking for a material based on its composition, but based on its properties. They will say, "I need something that does this." Or, "I need to be able to do this with it." The inquiries are not just about what something is composed of...

KD …but rather what conversation they can have with it. If they push on it, how is it going to talk back to them.

MP Exactly. And that is not unusual because we are dealing with materials that have many attributes. Right now we are working on, in collaboration with the Harvard Graduate School of Design, a shared, open database and taxonomy, meaning that when you look up a material you will see where it can be found. We are anticipating that art schools and engineering schools across the country will engage in the project, registering the materials that they have.

KD And will the taxonomies developed for the database be quite different from the common composition and properties search fields?

MP Yes. This database will take into account sourcing. It will incorporate new tools, such as geographical information. For example, we have the location information for all the vendors we work with, and we will be able to say whether a certain company is a manufacturing location or a distribution location. So, if somebody wants to see materials local to a certain region, they will be able to understand what materials are made nearby versus what is just distributed nearby. We will also capture, through social media tools, the experiences people have with materials. Students will learn from the various degrees of success of others' shared experiences. Also, if there is a video of a material with 100 pounds of pressure on it, for example—maybe a student or the manufacturer made that resource—that will be linked and made available. Another thing I should point out is that everything circulates. That's extremely unusual for material collections, but we need to get materials into the hands of the students.

Fig. 37
Diana Wagner, *Oh Snap: Material Transformation + Attachments*, 2012

KD And into their studios where they can work with them.

MP Yes, and this is because we need our students to have advanced material literacy—including everything from the formal understanding of materials to an appreciation of the life cycle and environmental impact concerns

in relationships between materials. For instance, if a student has a project dealing with children's furniture, maybe human toxicity is a big concern and environmental impact is a little lower on that list of concerns. But the key is in understanding where their material choices and selections fit in. The way that we teach students how to do research, the way we teach them visual literacy, and the way that we recognize how they learn apply to materials in a way that is unique to RISD because of all the different departments that we serve.

KD That is one of the things that is exciting about the new database. Sourcing information and sharing people's experience with others will be huge components. The library is hosting this shared, open resource to help anyone engage in conversations with a network of materials. Why have we not had material collections like this accessible in libraries before?

MP I think we can call it a "post-digital" phenomenon. We got used to digital files, but now there is a return to "stuff," an appreciation of it, especially in the current context of accelerating innovation. I recently attended a symposium about material science education and a presenter stated, and I paraphrase but the concept is the same: in 1900, there were something like 200 materials known in the world, but since 1950 we have seen 200,000 materials accessed and labeled. That incredible upward trend is accelerating. The idea that students are fabricating materials further creates an expectation for a collection and database to handle that appropriately. I don't think there are many collections in which it is planned that student-generated content is going to be acquired in the same way as content is acquired from production companies.

KD Yes, this recognizes that solutions come from many places. And that experimental, pre-production materials are important. Companies often want students, the next generation of researchers, to have access to the materials that the company or research team is developing. But this is different—the MRC will provide access to student-made materials as well.

MP Yes. The way that people are coming in to the MRC makes me feel satisfied that we built something that people can respond to. Some types of engagement are formal—somebody just wants to use a material for a design project. Others are really about exploring the idea of what that material is about, approaching the collection as an incubator or inspiration lab.

KD It makes me think about something Jocelyne said, that materials have their own vocabularies.

MP Yes, and personalities. As we see how people work with materials and what their experiences are, the materials' personalities emerge.

The stakes of these conversations are significant. Material negotiations play a major role in social infrastructure, political practice, personal being, the environment, and the aesthetics and ethics of engagement. Today, we are able to work with materials and craft at scales ranging from the global and atmospheric to the molecular and atomic. Nanoparticle and quantum computing research currently offer dramatic and promising insights into material behaviors and possibilities for human benefit. Even at the tiniest of scales, through scanning electron microscopy and the use of the smallest of reaction chambers, the human-to-material composite relationship and collaboration is of an imaginative, physical, and energetic space that we know in some ways already. As high-tech material manipulation tools become more widely accessible, it is important that artists and designers meet this opportunity with an ever-deepening understanding of material in general and of the specific materials that we work with in particular. As we develop the skill of "listening" to materials, observing them far beyond their surface properties, we also develop our liveliness and deeply engaged perception and action. We meet a material with force and it replies back with force: we work, we make something, we change.

How might this reciprocal way of working with materials extend to a broad range of habitual, personal, social, political, and environmental engagements and processes? Gottfried Leibniz, famous as the father of calculus, suggests a role model. Leibniz's genius was in his ability to observe, empathize, and enter into collaboration with materials often at scales beyond what was accessible through optical vision and scientific measurement tools of the time. Leibniz's insights into structures and rational access to matter, and his abilities to translate these into mathematical theorems and invent applicable languages, are tied directly to his experiences with materials at hand. He developed differential calculus, composed the *Discourse on Metaphysics* (1686), and worked on diplomatic strategy for the House of Hannover and on reconciliation between the Catholic and Protestant churches, all during intense years in the Harz mountains of Germany, where most of his time and efforts went into developing mechanisms to harness wind power for the silver mines.[3] He was deeply interested in channeling the energy of wind and water in the most efficient way possible—something we are still struggling to do today. He was drawn to work directly with materials. He knew intimately that it is a matter of understanding the materials on their levels of being. He observed the land and its component parts intimately and intensely. He believed, as he explained in *The Monadology*, that every minute particle of matter, the most minute, the most elemental, has in its being the potential, the ability, the knowledge, and the code to become anything that matter can become, and to do anything that matter can do.

An understanding for this kind of perspective is possible when we allow our imaginations to enter, empathically, into the material. These examples of perceiving community with material counter much of mainstream human production of material things. Indeed, material awareness is often approached with an anxious ambivalence. Pervasive pollutants, hormone interrupters, and energy resource depletion show the imbalance of material use. Global environmental and governmental instabilities draw attention to complex forces intermixed in material, personal, social, and political composition. New ways of perceiving render previously overlooked connections. Materials can push and pull, organize, help form culture, and are vital, lively participants in everything. Materials are effective and affective; they have creative capacity to make something new occur or appear, and to alter what is already there. It is possible for people to grow this broad sense of communication with the materials they come into dialogue with. This optimistic belief enters social consciousness periodically, and it is here now. As we shift our attitudes toward materials dramatically in the present and near future, we will shift our understandings of what it is to be human. By directing imaginative, sensory attention toward the possibilities already in materials themselves as they strive to communicate, we open ourselves to essential benefits—if we let ourselves listen. What is happening when we meet material with empathetic imagination? What is happening if we do not?

Notes

1. Gottfried Wilhelm Freiherr von Leibniz, *The Principles of Philosophy, or, the Monadology* (1714), in *Discourse on Metaphysics & Other Essays*, trans. Daniel Garber and Roger Ariew (Indianapolis: Hackett Publishing Company, Inc., 1991), 68, 71.

2. See especially Phil Howes and Zoe Laughlin, *Material Matters: New Materials in Design* (London: Black Dog Publishing, 2012); Mike Ashby and Kara Johnson, *Materials and Design: The Art and Science of Material Selection in Product Design* (Oxford, UK: Butterworth-Heinemann, 2002); and Blaine Brownell, ed., *Transmaterial 3: A Catalog of Materials That Redefine Our Physical Environment* (New York: Princeton Architectural Press, 2010).

3. See Gottfried Wilhelm Freiherr von Leibniz, *Protogaea*, trans. and eds. Claudine Cohen and Andre Wakefield (Chicago: University of Chicago Press, 2008).

Graphic Design, Storytelling, and the Making of Meaning

Lucinda Hitchcock

How do critical makers transform today's vast proliferation of information into meaningful visual culture? Lucinda Hitchcock, Professor, Graphic Design, provides a glimpse into her discipline, describing graphic designers as today's scribes and illuminators, as curators and storytellers, and as keen observers of and participants in the making of cultural meaning. Outlining how the Graphic Design department prepares its graduates to shape the future of information design and visual communication, she describes the elements of type, narrative, and visual linguistics that students form and transform in becoming uniquely inventive thinkers and makers.

It's an understatement of course to say that information is everywhere. But it is, and more than ever information has become the currency (as well as the burden) of our times. Since the earliest days of the Renaissance, society's most literate individuals—the scribes, illuminators, printers, and bookmakers—have been sorting out how to present and disseminate information in all its forms. Indeed, for as long as there has been an audience capable of reading and affording information, there have been craftspeople dedicated to organizing and presenting the visually complex content of culture.

One could argue that today's graphic designers are cultural curators. We condense society's stories visually—choosing, framing, and presenting what gets seen, reproduced, and disseminated. We organize visual information, shaping complex economic arguments in the form of graphs, charts, maps, and diagrams; we create books, newspapers, websites, and exhibitions. Graphic designers organize and arrange signage, wayfinding systems, commercial spaces, and web spaces. We design learning materials, voter forms, schedules for transit systems, and calendars. We produce charts and medical information and develop brand identity systems. We design user interfaces and interactive experiences. We work with urban planners and new-media developers. Wherever there is information to be presented, spatial environments that need navigating, or written language, form, and image working together in concert, you can be sure a graphic designer is involved.

The term "graphic designer" was coined in the 1920s by William Addison Dwiggins, a prominent book designer best known for the work he did for Alfred Knopf, publisher. Historians say that Dwiggins came up with the term in order to distinguish his activities from that of others dabbling in the typographic arts.[1] Like many of today's multi-skilled designers, Dwiggins was a Renaissance man, designing all manner of things, from books to lampshades, typefaces to marionettes, calligraphy to book bindings. He embraced new technologies while enthusiastically honoring the sheer aesthetic beauty of abstract graphical decoration. He revived the art of book design in America and placed Knopf on the map for the sheer excellence of their book production. Like others in his cohort of early- to mid-century American graphic designers—Lester Beall, Bradbury Thompson, and Paul Rand come to mind—Dwiggins was a practical modernist who emerged from the Arts and Crafts era with as much interest in decoration and play as in pragmatic purposefulness.

As diverse as Dwiggins and his contemporaries' practices were, graphic designers of the last century were not called on to be as flexible as today's young graphic designers. They had the luxury of time and stillness, and could focus more on the minutiae of their craft. The scope of graphic design then was arguably simpler: surfaces were largely two-dimensional and paper based, and the tasks at hand were perhaps clearer. The absence of motion and screens, digital technology and social media, or even academic programs in graphic design meant the graphic designer's role was narrower compared to today, and relatively unexamined. Notions of "interface design" and "experience design" had yet to surface, and the designer's job was largely about the conjunction of type, image, presentation, and message.

Ever since "graphic designer" came into common use, designers have argued over its ability to accurately describe what it is we do. The term is especially uncomfortable for some practitioners today, as the boundaries of the field continue to expand. Today's graphic designer is a different animal, responsible for so much more territory. With this increase in responsibility comes added awareness of, and accountability for, the power of visual media itself, more theoretical introspection, and far more reflection on what it is we do and how we define ourselves. The more recent, and possibly more descriptive term used to define our field—"visual communication design"—has been adopted by many academic institutions in recent years. While the term might relinquish historical ties to our graphic design predecessors, it nevertheless accurately describes an opening of boundaries as the designer's turf widens.

That openness is evident in RISD's Graphic Design department. Nomenclature aside, those who go through RISD's program might feel entirely comfortable working in computational programming, user-experience design, public art, data visualization, type design, exhibition design, "environmental graphic design," book binding, and so on, often simultaneously. A student doing a typography assignment might end up projecting transit schedules onto bus shelters. Others (Emmi Laakso and Robin Davis, both BFA 2011 Graphic Design) might transform an institutional disagreement within the school into a performance piece with life-preservers spelling out prophetic slogans floating on the canal (fig. 38). The careful observation of a singular object—a lock of hair from a nineteenth-century poet for example, found at the John Hay Library at Brown University up the hill—might become a jump-ing off point for an intensive study of the grotesque, leading a student (Jerel Johnson, MFA 2014 Graphic Design) to the Nature Lab, where insects' parts are scanned at an incredibly high resolution and turned into posters via an automatic scripting device (fig. 39). A project prompt which leads a student (Kai Salmela, BFA 2006 Graphic Design) to understand the history of our own Market Square results in a large-scale projection that shows thousands of hatch marks indicating the number of slaves who were moved through Rhode Island's ports (fig. 40).

Bearing in mind this confluence of considerations—the past, with its rich histories of typography, print, language, and reproduction processes; the present, with its insistence on multidisciplinarity and technological literacy; and the future, whose aspect is increasingly less predictable but certainly more expansive than ever before—we in the Graphic Design department at RISD enjoy the challenges inherent in staying current and are continuously engaged in reflecting upon and reviewing our curriculum. In this climate of constant change, we remain agile and adaptable, and yet some of our depart-ment's goals have remained essentially the same for more than 20 years, a fact we point to with a good deal of pride. Pedagogically, we work to guide our students toward engaged, conscientious, and socially connected learning while giving them the skills to *see* through *making*. Students exercise their hands and their eyes from the moment they join our department, always

Fig. 38
Emmi Laakso and
Robin Davis, *Sink or
Swim*, 2011

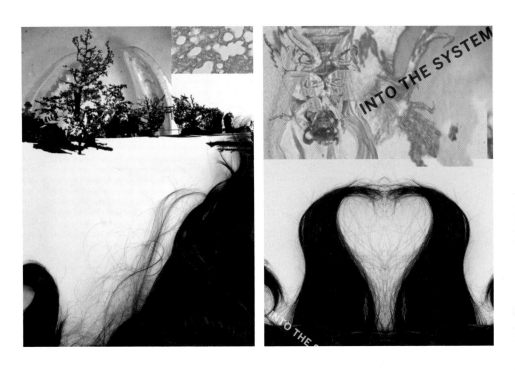

Fig. 39
Jerel Johnson,
Grotesque, 2012

considering the relationship between meaning, form, method, and tool. We guide them to become confident in communication theory and design methods, to decipher and unpack all manner of visual language, and to author and make work with various points of view. We see strength in breadth as well as depth, in the search as well as the discovery.

Perhaps most of all, we foster an ability to think through the *narrative* of a design problem, for regardless of the historical, cultural, and technological moment, the one timeless task that we graphic designers are all charged with is the telling of stories. While a graphic designer's stories might not begin with "once upon a time," we nevertheless use many of the same tools and techniques that writers might use. Like a writer, the conscientious graphic designer gives thoughtful attention to the beginning, middle, and end. A graphic designer considers the frame, the details, and the point of view of each and every visual moment and weighs every dot, line, word, pixel, and image that is put to work to express a point, strike a particular tone, or reach a designated "reader."

It goes without saying that without a reader, or audience, there can be no communication. And like any teller of stories, a graphic designer must consider and hold the attention of an audience, focusing on how delivery and distribution takes place. The designer strives for aptness and believability among audiences. For example, a designer would be unlikely to use

Fig. 40
Kai Salmela,
*Market House
Hatchmarks,*
2006

a woodcut illustration when designing a complex and authoritative infographic—unless of course the designer were purposefully investigating the properties of "infographic-ness" (which is, ironically, just the kind of thing that happens at RISD all the time). At RISD, such an exercise might lead to a fruitful discussion about objectivity, subjectivity, and universality in imagery and media. Foremost in the discussion would be an effort to unpack the goal of a design's intended use in the first place. Style conveys meaning just as much as material and craft. An emergency "EXIT" sign spray-painted in green paint using a loopy hand-drawn script on a piece of recycled cardboard might be pretty but would fail to convey the authority that such a sign requires. People wouldn't recognize it—they wouldn't *believe* in it. And it likely wouldn't save them in the event of a fire. An overly detailed or excessively ornate icon intended for use on an iPhone or tablet would fail in its intention to simply and clearly communicate the "story" of the app for which it serves as a signpost or stand-in.

A graphic designer also shares storytelling techniques with the filmmaker, considering, for example, the mise en scène—"the arrangement of actors and scenery on a stage for a theatrical production," as Webster's defines it. On stage, a director dictates the relational dynamics between actors and set and audience. A designer developing any sort of user interface must also consider the entire scene: How does a tool get used? Where and when is it used? What is the context for use? What are the obstacles? A designer of two-dimensional printed messages, or even of large-scale sign systems, must consider context too. How fast does a driver move past a traffic sign, for example? At what speed can the sign still be legible? What do pedestrians see differently from drivers? All these factors play into how the "story" is framed and delivered. The story is always being served, even if it is as simple as "this way to the nearest off-ramp."

In simple terms, a story is a stand-in or substitute for an event itself. Surrounding any story are the metaphors, tropes, and stylistic devices that make a story more compelling, more understandable, or more contextually relevant to the listener or reader. Likewise, graphic design often produces designed elements that are stand-ins or substitutes for that which cannot be present. A logo is a story that stands in for a company. A picture is a story that stands in for reality. A symbol is a story that represents a larger idea or belief. Such "stories" can be as brief as a simple mark or as complex as an overarching identity system that brands a complex organization or corporation. A story can include not only the content or "point," but also the entirety of its extenuating framework. So, for example, the story of let's say a postage stamp includes not only the design or image on its surface along with its currency designation, it also includes the paper it's printed on, the people who did the printing, the glue, the person who licked the stamp, the envelope it ends up on, the letter in the envelope, and the mail slot it might pass through. Follow this thread and it can be endless. And yet it is exactly this trajectory—of production, use, and distribution—that makes up the whole story of the postage stamp. These are the "stories," with all the potential relationships that occur between each stage, that the designer must consider before setting out to shape experience.

Graphic design is the perfect discipline for anyone interested in the convergence of visual form, concept, and story. In my own case it was a perfect fit, not so much because of some early proclivity toward graphic image making, but rather because of my affinity for stories, words, and language. I was an English major and also received a master's degree in literature before switching careers. I simply loved anything to do with books. Letters. Words. Stories. Grammar. Bindings. Paper. Type. I was then, and still am, a true believer in the power of books (and words for that matter) to transport. And I've always been fascinated by the intricacies of story *telling*—the *how* of the story as well as the *what*. In grad school, and before shifting careers, I developed my interest in literary theory (form) and analysis of story (content). I was drawn to the critical and analytic dissection of plot structures and enjoyed investigating and exposing an author's narrative devices. After a several-year stint in the book industry, I went on to study graphic design in earnest and received my MFA degree at Yale University, where my thesis work, *Visual Poetics: Towards an Understanding of Words in Space*, primed me for teaching at a school like RISD, where a theoretical, conceptual, *and* pragmatic way of looking at the discipline is embraced.

In the RISD Graphic Design undergraduate program, students progress in their three years from the formal aspects of visual storytelling to the development of more complex and conceptual messages and user experiences. Sophomore courses focus on developing a student's skill in the formal and compositional parts of storytelling (the grammar or syntax), while more advanced classes prompt students to play out more complex narratives (the semantics or meaning). To tell a story visually, students learn how to recognize, manipulate, and control the intricacies of visual language. This involves all manner of design skills, processes, and methodologies, including but not limited to: framing, composing, persuading, directing, curating, designating, organizing, sequencing, conducting, condensing, translating, printing, drawing, reading, and writing. This list, though long, is still (and to some extent always will be) incomplete, because the discipline of graphic design, like the term itself, has out of necessity remained elastic. It evolves as culture, commerce, information, and communication evolve—and attendant modes of making and educating evolve too.

In Graphic Design, our "core courses" (supported by a wide variety of electives) are the basis for teaching students to interpret, frame, and present complex ideas in visually accessible forms. Typography—the arrangement of language and letterforms—is the first part of the core sequence, and taught through all three years of the major. An essential tool in the forming of language, typography—defined by Robert Bringhurst as "the craft of endowing human language with a durable visual form"—is almost exclusively the turf of graphic designers, our lifeblood, if you will.[2] Whether on paper, on screens large or small, in interior spaces, or highway signs, to name just a few examples, designers and typographers orchestrate a correct balance between appropriate typeface, elegance, clarity, and cohesion with other visual elements. We maintain and pass judgment on issues of legibility, grace, and functionality, combining type with image, form, and space.

When learning typography, students are first introduced to the Roman alphabet and its history and evolution, especially in the development of communication, literacy, and printing. They learn that as writing systems developed, letters evolved from ideograms (symbols that contain meaning) to phonograms (marks that convey sound). This knowledge opens up a whole new understanding about how letterforms in and of themselves convey a kind of meaning, even before being gathered into words, sentences, paragraphs, and pages. Students go on to learn the characteristics of certain typeface classification systems developed in the past five centuries and begin to understand the taxonomies and nomenclature of typography. They learn about the structure and architecture of letterforms, how to create legible and aesthetically appropriate compositions with typography, and to begin seeing that letters and textual material have form and counter-form (figure and ground) (see fig. 41; Lauren Sun, BFA 2009 Graphic Design). Indeed, we teach that conceptually and formally, the art of typography is truly the art of understanding how *space* works to support the conveyance of meaning.

Later in the type curriculum, students analyze and use different typographic techniques in various media (books, film, web, and handheld devices) and through various platforms (digital, letterpress, and handlettering) and learn to consider context, use, and situation and how they invariably influence typographic choices. One significant project asks students to produce a typographic reading experience in the form of a book. Given a text, for example Marguerite Duras's *Writing* or Thomas Pynchon's *Crying of Lot 49*, they are asked to consider the content carefully and then bring to the reading experience a second or even third typographic voice/text of their own choosing, to subvert, support, comment on, or refute the original text. They must figure out, with all the grace and elegance available in the typographic tradition, how to create a *new* reading experience that allows a reader to digest the original text while also appreciating the inter-textual commentary and a nontraditional typographic environment. The results are complex, beautiful, and truly push the boundaries of how we define text in the first place. And of course the students must also print, bind, and produce in multiple copies a small edition (see fig. 42; Aaron Shoon, MFA 2006 Graphic Design).

Typography is about more than just its conventional appearance and choices of font or size or color. Typography is concerned with context, location, surface, user, dimension, and material. So, for example, look around you for some type. Some words—on a sign, a sticker, a poster, this book,

Fig. 41
Lauren Sun, "Type
History" project, 2007

Fig. 42
Aaron Shoon, "Type 2"
book project, 2005

BGK
SUW
5678?
efgrtuy

Franklin Gothic No. 2 Roman
TYPOGRAPHY

Helvetica
TYPOGRAPHY

Univers 55 Roman
TYPOGRAPHY

News Gothic Medium
TYPOGRAPHY

anything. Ask yourself: How is it produced? Is it printed with ink, written by hand, or digital? Is it carved in stone or made out of light and pixels? Is the typography (not the words themselves, but the typography) informing, directing, manipulating, or emoting? Is it utilitarian, expensive, formal, or "vernacular"? Does it reveal itself over time or can it be absorbed and comprehended in a single momentary glance? How do you respond to words that are small, printed, and familiar, versus words that are very large, or carved into stone, or in some way monumental? What happens when conventional forms are subverted to convey unconventional messages? We are all used to the little stickers we see on fruit at the grocery store, for example. But what if one day, instead of the usual identification numbers, the bananas you bought had something else stuck to their skins? Little poems perhaps, or texts about child labor in banana plantations? Wasily Davidov (BFA 2005 Graphic Design) sculpted the word "OUCH" and squeezed it between two buildings on RISD's campus that were soon to be dramatically transformed (fig. 43). This placement was critical to how a reader received the information. Considering such scenarios, you are performing a fundamental research task that becomes second nature to our students—a brief critical analysis of typography, contextual signs, intentions, and even narrative.

Most core courses in the department's line-up focus on narrative—the structure and manner of presenting story or idea; and visual linguistics—the grammar and mechanics of (visual) language and how it is disseminated and received. The curriculum thus leads from type classes and "Form and Communication" through "Making Meaning," "Color," "Visual Systems," "Relational Design," and finally "Degree Project." While each course has its own particular focus, with parameters appropriate to the development of the students, all the classes are profoundly interconnected, all focus on determining the need within a given design situation, and all privilege the story, the message, and the *meaning* to be conveyed.

In "Form and Communication," students explore how certain visual modes affect meaning and its reception. One project asks students to design

Fig. 43
Wasily Davidov,
OUCH, 2005

Fig. 44
Rebecca Zhang,
pictograms, 2012

a pictogram for five areas of campus: the auditorium, the museum, health services, the library, and the cafeteria (fig. 44; Rebecca Zhang, BFA 2015 Graphic Design). A pictogram is a utilitarian mark that is used in a variety of ways: in signage, in print, on screen, and in mobile devices. Pictograms may seem simple on the surface, but they are much more complex when you consider the ramifications of making and using them. A pictogram is to a detailed drawing what a haiku is to a novel. It is reduced to its simplest possible representation—and made up of simple, clear, and objective forms. Much goes into that reduction, and when it is done well, the images are poetic, brief, and beautiful. In class, pictograms prompt us to ask: How can an icon hold just enough but not too much meaning for the brief and immediate read it provokes? How can a simple mark represent not only a place but also the experience of that place? And how can formal decisions be made to carry through an entire system of pictograms?

Now, to understand how form (composition, mode, and media) and communication (story, intention, and message) actually work, imagine this simple example: Picture a set of instructions—something ordinary perhaps, like the IKEA diagrams that come with furniture assembly instructions. Think about that white sheet of paper, with its unembellished, utilitarian, black-and-white images, whose sole purpose is to be accurate, comprehensible, and useful. These kinds of diagrams are made mechanically, drawn to look precise and objective and to impart extremely clear information. Now imagine those same diagrams created in a different way, perhaps with the rough line quality of a woodcut. Or picture them painted in soft watercolors. How would you feel about the diagrams then? Would they still be diagrams? Would they be beautiful? Useful? Meaningful? Easier or more difficult to follow? Occasionally students question this seemingly objective nature of diagrams and line work and use them instead to subvert the notion of truth, complicating an idea purposefully to achieve a deliberate or poetic ambiguity. Indeed, sometimes a situation calls for a viewer to spend a bit more time with a visual message—to *not* absorb or comprehend it instantaneously (see fig. 45; Jessica Greenfield, MFA 2011 Graphic Design).

RISD's graphic design students learn to consciously and critically parse such details. They become aware that not all lines are created equal. A vector line carries with it its own DNA, its own code for expressing meaning and inviting interpretation, while a hand-drawn line carries a distinctly different code and a different set of meanings. A woodcut *means* something—the mode itself carries a story, a vestige of the process that made it. The hand is in evidence. It evokes time, history, and tradition. It highlights a link between the process and the image, between the tools chosen to cut the surface and the final result. The contrastingly thin and ordinary vector lines of diagrammatic language carry the authority of "rightness." They are "correct." Objective. True. There is very little nuance in a diagram, just pure functionality. These visual and formal distinctions evolve over time, derived through context and social agreement, and from consistent application and use.

"Making Meaning," another core, indeed signature course, explores the essential nature of graphic design and directly introduces the notion that storytelling, or "narrative," is a large part of the design enterprise. "Making Meaning" has evolved over many years. While always studio-based, it

V.I.S.I.B.I.L.I.T.Y

A well designed object divulges its INNER WORKINGS

EMPATHY

To use a tool YOU MUST INHABIT IT

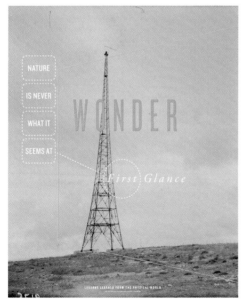

NATURE

IS NEVER

WHAT IT

SEEMS AT

WONDER

First Glance

CONSISTENCY

repetition

fosters

curiosity

and

understanding

was initially theory-driven, focused on models and methods derived from C.S. Pierce's semiotics. Today, it includes a basic introduction to semiotics principles and linguistic theory. The class addresses image-making, framing, and introductory film theory along with the dynamics of type, form, and image. Students work on projects that uncover the distinctions between denotation and connotation and learn to manipulate the visual representation of objectivity and subjectivity. The class is concerned with context, concept, and story, and students are taught to control visual narrative using sequence, photography, and motion. Semantics (meaning), syntactics (form, visual grammar, and the arrangement of elements), and pragmatics (use, practicality, function) are principal tenets. Assignments incorporate concepts such as point-of-view, communication design, and sequence in the act of visual storytelling.

In one assignment, for example, students are asked to develop a strong visual message in the form of a poster about a chosen social issue. Students begin this project with a topic in mind (access to healthy food, climate change, representations of women, and so on) and explore imagery that addresses their chosen areas subjectively, objectively, and even idiosyncratically. They are also asked to write texts that are likewise objective, subjective, and idiosyncratic to accompany the images. The merging of the images and text *is* the design process, and a meaningful one. After several weeks of this critical-thinking stage, students usually arrive at a clearer position on their subject matter and go on to produce powerful, emotional, and informative posters (see fig. 46; Micah Barrett, BFA 2012 Graphic Design).

Another introductory "Making Meaning" exercise involves the deceptively simple task of pairing an image with a word. Students are given a long list of well-known photographers (Dorothea Lange, Robert Frank, Diane Arbus, Richard Avedon, Walker Evans, and others). Each student also receives three or four words from a magnet poetry set. The physicality of these words is important. I ask them to spend some time in the library looking closely at the photographers' work on the list. Once they choose an

Fig. 45
Jessica Greenfield,
*Lessons Learned
from the Physical
World*, 2010

Feeding America
23.5
MILLION
AMERICANS
GET THEIR
FOOD
FROM
CONVENIENCE
STORES &
GAS
STATIONS

image, they must select a word or two from among the ones they've received, and simply situate the word(s) on the same surface as the image, with only a scant consideration of placement or "design." They then photocopy the arrangement. Once they have that completed, they take their word-and-image composition and blow it up to poster size. The results are fascinating. A well-known image (think of Arbus's image *Child with Toy Hand Grenade*) with, say, the word "Suddenly" or "Mother" placed within the frame, is utterly altered by the inclusion of the text. The project leads to rich conversations about how meaning is derived from images, the relationship of word to image, and the power of word over image, or vice versa.

"Relational Design" follows on "Making Meaning." Here, students focus on collaborative learning and explore how new media and evolving technologies can serve social as well as informational needs. One remarkable project asks students to invent a new machine or automated process that alters or replaces a typically human-controlled action. They soon discover that the meaning of an object resides not only in its primary use, but in the way that it encourages interaction or collaboration, or even how it might open space for other activities. A newfangled book-binding machine, for example, might simplify a task that design students are often consumed with. While a machine might offer a shortcut to a fairly craft-heavy activity, it also allows for new interactions and discoveries, becoming a device for gathering and connecting not only pages but people.

The senior year for a graphic design student opens up significantly. Students immerse themselves in mature, research-oriented, independent projects that are often astoundingly intelligent and culminating proof of years of simultaneous thinking and making. One project that stands out is that of Nicole Poor (BFA 2011 Graphic Design), who devised an analysis of the three "books" with the largest print run in the world: the Bible, *Harry Potter*, and the IKEA catalog. With deadpan elegance, she derived a series of iterations of a single page from each. From the Bible, she chose page one of Genesis. From *Harry Potter* she chose the copyright page. And from the IKEA catalog,

Fig. 46
Micah Barrett,
Feeding America,
2009

she chose the "sofa info" page. Taking these pages as starting points, she made her own interpretive designs, and developed an entirely new meaning, not only from the individual works but from the collective act of using them for a new purpose—for *her* purpose. In one bold conceptual move she made a statement about mass production, publishing, consumerism, and conformity *and* generated a unique artwork that completely contradicted notions of conformity.

Graduate students at RISD come from a variety of backgrounds. Some have BFAs in graphic design and participate in a two-year track, while others have degrees in science, literature, art, or engineering, to name a few, and take part in a three-year track. Together, these students form a powerful brain trust of ideas and techniques for visualizing meaning. Graduate projects that stand out run the gamut, from Wael Morcos's (MFA 2013 Graphic Design) visual and typographic translation/reinterpretation of Alan Lightman's *Einstein's Dreams* (fig. 47), to Colin Frazer's (MFA 2013 Graphic Design) *World Wide Web Wilderness*, a site that asks visitors to click on a Paypal button to contribute to the preservation of a virtual wilderness, but where, critically, nothing actually takes place. In 2011, the graduating MFA students decided to present their thesis exhibition in the form of a free newspaper rather than adapt to the "white cube" of the fine art realm. The low-budget printed piece, in stark black, white, and red, along with an accompanying web site, became both a repository for individual projects and a collective, public gesture (fig. 48). As they wrote: "This is the catalog of the show, which is also the show. It is a collection of work from our individual thesis investigations; an index of the physical gallery space; and a record of our collaborative process. The show is a unified work that extends beyond the exhibition space and hinges on its distribution. The work is not complete until it enters circulation."

It may be clear by now that graduate theses, and indeed many undergraduate degree projects, tread a fine line between pragmatic "design" and work we might more readily identify as conceptual art. This very blur is

Fig. 47
Wael Morcos, *Einstein's Dreams* project, 2012

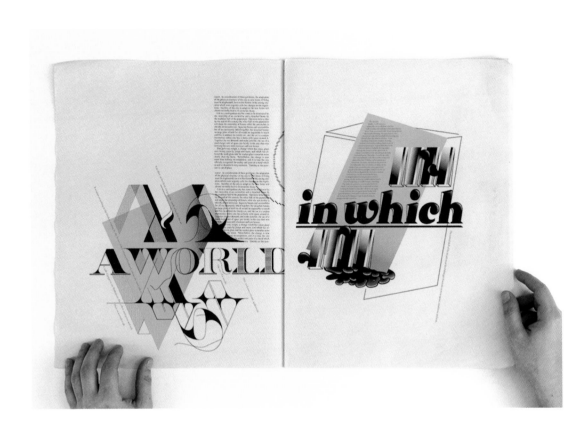

perhaps what we're most proud of. Our educational goal is not just to shape the development of a graphic designer per se, but to help shape a whole person who is adept in thinking, making, and seeing and equipped to engage critically in conveying stories and making meaning. We are not interested in teaching a particular set of skills, nor in graduating young designers with a "RISD-style" portfolio. On the contrary, when a RISD student can show, after a few years of critical, conscientious making, that they can engage graphic design tools and processes to author their own positions in service of making information and ideas meaningful, then we know we have done our job.

Notes

1. Steven Heller, *Typographic Treasures: The Work of W. A. Dwiggins* (New York: ITC Corporation, 1986), 3.

2. Robert Bringhurst, *The Elements of Typographic Style*, 1st edition (Vancouver: Hartley and Marks, 1992), 111.

Fig. 48
MFA Graphic Design
Class of 2011,
*This Is the Catalog
of the Show*, 2011

The Nature Imperative

Neal Overstrom

How does nature inform artists and designers today? And
how is nature, as seen through the eyes of critical makers,
becoming increasingly relevant far beyond the realm of art
and design? Neal Overstrom, Director of RISD's Nature Lab,
describes this beloved resource—established in 1937 by artist
and faculty member Edna Lawrence—as offering not only
inspiration through nature's forms, but a crucial context for
exploring, interpreting, and sharing the essential human-
nature connection and its potential for artists and designers.

Walking into the Nature Lab at Rhode Island School of Design is like stepping into a Victorian cabinet of curiosities. Worn floorboards creaking underfoot, we're surrounded by wood and glass cabinets brimming with taxidermic birds and mammals, vertebrate bones, dried plants and seeds, mollusk shells, marine corals, and other such artifacts from the living world. Head mounts of African and North American game animals peer down from above, butterflies in glass boxes form a colorful mosaic, and if we look carefully we might even find a winged rabbit tucked away on a shelf (fig. 49). In so many ways the space seems reminiscent of an era when natural history was a dominant field of science, Charles Darwin and Alfred Wallace advanced new ideas on the origins of life, and the notion prevailed that through careful collection, observation, and categorizing of specimens even laypeople could understand the relationships between living things and the processes of evolution.

Commenting on cabinets of curiosity that emerged from this era, evolutionary biologist Stephen Jay Gould once wrote, "I have long recognized the theory and aesthetic of such comprehensive display: show everything and incite wonder by sheer variety."[1] Wonder is indeed a typical response to the Nature Lab, but in the digital age natural history collections such as ours may seem anachronistic. Today, technology can deliver captivating images of the natural world in an instant, just as advances in molecular biology yield new tools for studying biodiversity. These developments have prompted many natural history museums to re-examine the significance and roles of their collections in research.[2] The Nature Lab, by contrast, has never been a more relevant resource for RISD's students and faculty. A site for many forms of observation and inquiry, it supports critically important education on hands-on learning, the subjectivity of "natural orders," biological influences on art and design, and art-science and human-nature connections.

Housed in RISD's Waterman Building, the first structure designed and constructed specifically for the school, the Nature Lab collection occupies a library and museum space that later became the classroom of long-time faculty member Edna Lawrence. Born in the New York City borough of Staten

Island in 1898, Lawrence attended RISD, graduating in 1920 and returning in 1922 to accept a faculty position that allowed her to grow as an artist and develop a style of realism in her paintings and drawings for which she would gain critical praise. Adventurous and with a keen interest in nature, Lawrence began in the 1920s and '30s what would become an annual ritual of summer—"sketching trips," camping her way by automobile across the United States or Canada one year, voyaging aboard export freighters to Europe or South America the next. By 1935 she had taken in the Canadian Maritimes, driven cross-country to California and back, and visited by ship many of the countries along the Mediterranean coast and the islands of the Caribbean. Each fall she returned to RISD to teach and share her experiences with students (fig. 50).

In 1937 the RISD library, then housed in Waterman, moved to a new location on campus. Lawrence and two other faculty members began assembling a materials-research laboratory in the newly vacated space, gathering industrial products, textile samples, and most significantly, natural history objects for students to use in her nature drawing class, a requirement for all freshmen. Thus, beginning with her own specimens, Lawrence built a collection over four decades that today numbers tens of thousands of objects acquired through other museums, donated from personal collections, or collected by Lawrence herself. Since Lawrence's retirement in 1977, curators with expertise in biology and science have managed the collection and continued her vision.

Fig. 49
Edna Lawrence
Nature Lab

Hands-on Learning and Personal Taxonomies

There are many reasons why the Nature Lab thrives but foremost is that it is neither an exhibition space nor a scientific research collection; it is a teaching collection and lending library where specimens can be removed from their cabinets, touched, examined, and even loaned out for detailed study in the dormitory room or studio. Staffed by work-study students and open 80 hours per week, the lab circulates more than 7,000 specimens each year to

individual students and faculty. Therein lies the cornerstone of the Nature Lab experience: hands-on, unmediated access to authentic natural history specimens. As faculty member Juliette Simpson has noted, "Natural history museums can be disappointing in that every specimen is locked away in a protective glass case. But the Nature Lab truly embodies the spirit of a laboratory; every bird and skull and shell is available, approachable, [and] ready for interaction.... 'Nature' goes from abstraction to reality there because you are surrounded by it, immersed in it, in a way that is not often possible in an academic environment."[3]

A consequence of this hands-on approach is that the Nature Lab can also be a bit messy. The objects often require ongoing cleaning and sometimes replacement after exposure to charcoal, gouache, and modeling clay. During certain weeks of figure drawing each semester a squad of human skeletons is invariably found draped across tables and chairs or dangling from railings, fulfilling their duties in a variety of study poses that muscles and ligaments would surely not allow in a living person.[4] Drawing easels often cram the space and a web of extension cords feeding portable lamps crisscrosses the room. Comparing the Nature Lab with other campus spaces, RISD graduate and exhibit designer Margaret Middleton wrote of her fellow students, "They preferred the cluttered, noisier, grittier atmosphere of the Nature Lab. To them, the Nature Lab was much more accessible...the place is nearly always packed. And effortlessly: no programs, no big exhibitions, just old animal skulls and sea shells."[5] Tangible, dynamic, interactive—these qualities distinguish the Nature Lab from many other kinds of learning environments.

Another distinctive feature of the Nature Lab is that unlike most natural history museums the collection is not rigidly organized by taxonomy. Once-living specimens are only loosely divided by Kingdoms of Life and rocks and minerals are housed without specific reference to their geologic origins. In a sense the collection can be considered a composition, a place for visual experimentation. Plant seeds are often found arranged without consideration of evolutionary relationships but instead simply by size and shape. A drawer

Fig. 50
Edna W. Lawrence,
1951

filled with minerals is organized by color rather than other chemical or physical properties, anathema to a right-minded geologist. Edna Lawrence herself organized specimens in idiosyncratic ways, arranging samples in an odd assortment of boxes that once held sewing needles or typewriter ribbons to compose modest but thoughtful studies of symmetry, color, pattern, texture, and form (fig. 51).

Comparison, juxtaposition, and composition—all integral aspects of art and design—help students see myriad potential systems, a process that mirrors the way cognitive scientists believe the human brain organizes information and conceptualizes the world. Assemblages of objects represent physical manifestations of what has been referred to as the "collaging" process of the mind—with images, experiences, and ideas being sorted and configured in particular ways.[6] By simply arranging a group of objects, we connect deeply to how we learn and make meaning. In one Nature Lab workshop students are asked to divide a subset of the collection into categories based on any characteristics they consider significant. Sometimes this leads to similar outcomes, for instance when moths and butterflies are divided into their own groups. Other times, however, participants free themselves from identification to imagine other possible schemes—arranging things by size, texture, symmetry, or color—thereby overcoming existing knowledge to see things in new ways.

Contemporary artist Mark Dion has devoted much of his practice to rearranging and recasting natural history collections, exemplifying how such interventions can challenge our cultural views on how the world should be ordered and in turn validate multiple perceptions of order, expert and amateur alike.[7] This not only substantiates subjective points of view, but inspires investment. Amateurs, he argues, are "able to experience the enthusiasm and excitement about discovery, which really drives scientific inquiry and artistic passion, as well. They're able to make it their own in a way."[8] A recent Nature Lab workshop involving a large group of professional artists, designers, scientists, and scholars from the social sciences and humanities

Fig. 51
Edna Lawrence, compositions of seashells, 1952–1954

at the Nature Lab reminded us that the benefits of a fresh take are not only individual. Co-organizer and Furniture Design faculty member Christopher Rose observed that in seeing things in new ways collectively, "participants built knowledge together by taking part in negotiated learning activities, which emphasized discussion and agreement.... The process of learning was slowed down, allowing participants to avoid jumping to assumptions based on preconceived notions or perceptions when interpreting information; rather the process enabled a critical appreciation of the development of knowledge."[9]

Biological Guides: Inspiration and Innovation

Edna Lawrence once observed, "Nature has been the inspiration for the Arts through the history of man—cave paintings, structures, buildings...one can always turn to it as a source for ideas and inventions." Asked about the purpose of the Nature Lab, she stated it was to "open students' eyes to the marvels of beauty in nature...of forms, space, color, texture, design, and structure and to help them realize the functions and reasons for nature's creations."[10] Seventy-five years after its founding we still find students in Lawrence's former classroom quietly and intently sketching mammal skulls, bird feathers, or beetles, exploring those same fundamental elements of art, design, and aesthetics. Olivia Verdugo (MFA 2011 Graphic Design) was inspired by the Nature Lab's collection in creating her graduate thesis work (fig. 52). As she wrote, "There is a compositional grammar and an order underlying every aspect of the natural world, shaped by forces which act upon great and small alike. I am fascinated by the patterns that emerge from this grammar...rich surface designs emerge from microscopic studies of a common pigeon's feather; the behavior of particles in fluid dictates the framework for a generative computer applet; the study of symbiosis spawns a new form of book."[11]

Representations of nature in mythology, literature, art, and culture are evident throughout history. Animals in particular figure prominently in our symbolism, representing certain qualities. Through myth and story

Fig. 52
Olivia Verdugo,
Quiet Storms, 2011

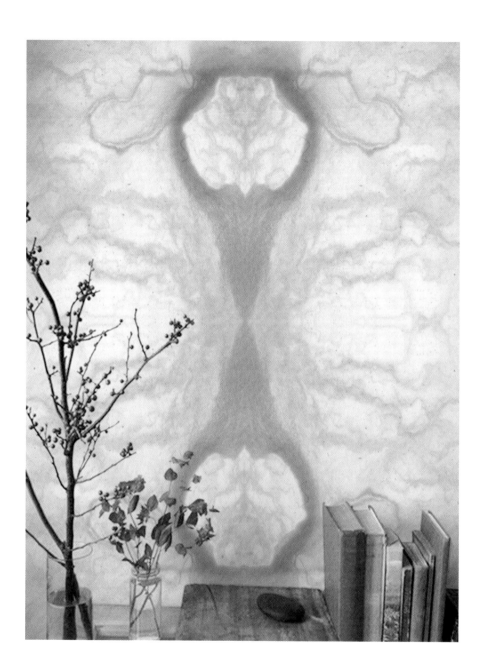

we have come to link owls with wisdom, foxes with cunning and trickery, butterflies with spirit and transformation. Zoe Wendel (BFA 2011 Jewelry + Metalsmithing) explored the symbolism of animals in her undergraduate work, drawing from two specimens in the Nature Lab's collection (figs. 53 and 54). Wendel's *Rabbit Skeleton* and *Spider Web* necklaces are an intriguing study in the mechanics of two very different organic structures, one fine and highly fluid and the other hard, jointed, and with limits to its motion. As she wrote, "The spider web was an exploration of gravity.... I imagined the thin silver chain replacing the spider's silken threads and how beautiful this would be in motion or draping across the body. The rabbit skeleton was also an exercise in gravity. I was drawn to [its] delicate shapes and forms and wanted to link the bones and put them in motion." But it was not just gravity that drew Wendel to nature, as she concludes, "I think it was the innate perfection in these objects."[12]

In the past decade or so biology has served as far more than symbolism and metaphor in the arts; it has brought growing awareness that the biological systems that evolved on Earth over the past 3.8 billion years can yield solutions to design problems of today. Janine Benyus's landmark 1997 book, *Biomimicry: Innovation Inspired by Nature*, catalyzed new thinking on ways to advance sustainable design by imitating or taking inspiration from nature's models. Advocates for a biomimetic approach to solving problems often start with the simple question: How would nature do it? One often cited example is the ventilation strategy of African termite mounds that allows the insects to maintain the internal temperature critical to growing the fungus on which they feed within a narrow range despite wide ranges of external temperatures. Applying the same principles to the design of buildings has demonstrated significant improvements in energy savings. Recent research into how certain butterflies' wings refract light with three-dimensional photonic crystals visible only at the nanoscale is fostering innovation in the development of more efficient solar energy cells and light emitting diodes.[13]

Figs. 53 and 54
Zoe Wendel, *Rabbit Skeleton Necklace*, 2010; *Spider Web Necklace*, 2010

Scientific Methods: Microscopy and Mental Imaging

In ecology—the study of the relationships between living organisms and their environments—the terms "edge effect" or "ecotone" are used to describe an area where two different habitat types or communities come together. The boundary between a forest edge and an open field is an example. Ecotones tend to sustain a high level of animal diversity as species exploit the benefits of both habitats with respect to food and shelter. In general, the more convoluted and entwined a boundary is the more animals tend to move across it. In a similar way the Nature Lab might be thought of as an ecotone, where topics related to the intersection of art, science, and research are increasingly explored and developed.

One way in which the Nature Lab is providing further engagement with science is by giving students expanded access to microscopes and microimaging systems. Over the past decade we have made significant investments in high-quality stereo and compound microscope systems, some outfitted with high-resolution, full-color cameras and fluorescence-imaging capacity. Microscopy has particular value for art and design students. First, as with nature history, microscopy is based principally on deep observation and therefore provides an intuitive portal to science consistent with other types of visual study. Second, microscopy provides students with access to myriad microscopic living specimens. The Nature Lab cannot maintain a large living collection, but just a single drop of pond water may contain bacteria, photosynthetic algae, predatory fish, invertebrate larvae, and many other living organisms that most students have never seen—an entire ecosystem full of a wondrous variety of forms, patterns, and structures.

Working with living specimens and microscopes, how would a laboratory exercise for art and design students differ from what we might find in a traditional science class? Further, what might the "two cultures" learn from one another? Those questions were the subject of a summer fellowship for RISD students Mengzhuo (Jenny) Li (BFA 2013 Apparel Design) and Eliza Squibb (BFA 2013 Textiles). Funded by the National Science Foundation through the

Rhode Island EPSCoR Academy (Experimental Program to Stimulate Competitive Research), their project involved developing and testing a classroom exercise featuring observation and discussion of microscopic specimens and academic research into the relationship between artistic and scientific inquiry, particularly focused on visualization and mental imaging.

Li and Squibb devised and subsequently tested a straightforward classroom exercise with professional K–12 educators from art, science, and humanities fields. Microscope stations were set up with living specimens including jellyfish-like ctenophores, juvenile fishes, phytoplankton, and sea stars. The teachers were asked to simply observe carefully, then to draw whatever they felt was interesting or significant, then to review the sketches as a group and divide them into categories based on the type of visual information they thought each communicated. A vigorous conversation ensued, much of it distinguishing between the artistic and the scientific, assessing the value or deficiencies of abstraction, and asking how realistic a drawing had to be to convey information. The final categories of images—labeled with words like "symmetry," "contour," and "texture"—were remarkably consistent with language that marine chemist James Mathewson used in defining a series of "master images" that he describes as the visual core of science, a reminder that both art and science are grounded in careful observation and visual inquiry (fig. 55).[14] The exercise was also a reminder that the type of collaborative assessment and dialogue common to studio critique in art and design may have broader application in other fields of education. One science educator noted: "Looking at all of the various depictions of marine life I found a particular question must be answered as a teacher: What does the student actually see? I can show him/her a picture but I don't know what he/she sees or thinks. Through collaboration the students can look at each other's work and find a consensual 'true view.'"[15]

At a summer conference with other undergraduate research fellows, Li and Squibb shared their insights on artistic and scientific inquiry.[16] Most significantly, they noted that visual imaging—the ability to think through

Boundary	Complement	Ordering	Space
Branching	Cycles	Packing	Strata
Chaos	Energetics	Path	Structure
Chirality	Flow	Point	Surface
Circuits	Folding	Polarity	Symmetry
Conduits	Gradients	Reflection	Time
Containers	Groups	Setting	Units
Coils	Magnitude	Shadows	Waves
Color	Motion	Signs	Webs

Fig. 55
James Mathewson's
"master images"
of science

images—was a key element for creativity in both the sciences and arts, along with other conceptual tools such as the ability to organize and express information through themes, metaphors, and analogies.[17] They cited studies showing that both imaging capacity and creativity are enhanced by artistic training.[18] Finally, they argued that additional visual training in science education could be beneficial to what has been described as the "art of the imagination," an elusive but crucial component of innovation practiced by visionary scientists from Galileo to Einstein.[19] Conversely, they reported that students in art and design schools may also see educational benefit in the integration of art and science curricula. Curriculum integration has been found to help students better connect new and existing knowledge and to foster relevance and meaning of this knowledge in student's lives.[20] Perhaps most significant, Li and Squibb pointed out that although we tend to perpetuate many preconceptions of a divide between "artist" and "scientist," there is mounting evidence that the "two culture debate" is more untrue now than ever.[21]

The Human-Nature Connection and Our Future

In 1984, biologist and conservationist E.O. Wilson published *Biophilia*, an influential book in which he explored the notion that humans have an innate affinity for life and life-like processes. Wilson and other proponents of this idea remind us that most of human evolution occurred in a bio-centric world in which our intellectual processes were inextricably linked to survival and reproduction. Just as certain nearly universal human phobias (such as a fear of snakes and insects) likely evolved to improve our ancestors' chances for survival, so too innate affinities for certain landscapes that offer security, elements such as plants and flowing water that offer nourishment, and spaces that reinforce our social connectivity could have helped humans survive as a species. Art philosopher Denis Dutton and others have even argued that art is a human need built into our DNA and our aesthetic perceptions are much more influenced by evolution than by culture.[22]

Though biophilia is considered a hypothesis, there is experimental evidence that our attraction for particular nature-related patterns, forms, and elements when represented in the built environment can have a significant impact on our physical and emotional well-being. For example, in an important 1984 study focused on health care settings, Roger Ulrich demonstrated that just having a view to a vegetated space out a hospital window shortened stays, reduced patients' needs for pain medications, and yielded fewer negative comments in nursing charts.[23] Subsequent research has consistently shown a link between stress reduction and exposure to nature or natural elements. It has even been shown that simply taking a lunch-time walk in a wooded park improves cognitive performance in office workers more so than a similar walk in a densely urban space.[24] It is this type of experimental evidence that points to our innate connection to the natural world and the importance of designing ways to better engage with nature in our daily lives.

Unfortunately there is also evidence that students coming to RISD and other schools today, though much more technologically literate, generally have much less exposure to nature growing up than those in earlier decades. In his book *Last Child in the Woods*, Richard Louv documented what he calls "nature-deficit disorder" to characterize the detrimental effects in children of having less contact with nature.[25] Louv argues that increased rates of

learning difficulties and childhood obesity are symptomatic of this shift and that children need more active contact with nature for healthy development. Designer Christina Kazakia (MID 2011 Industrial Design) wanted to be part of the movement to re-engage children with outdoor activities. Her thesis, "Natural Imagination: Reconnecting Urban Children with Nature," focused on creating a catalyst that would encourage children in urban areas to play outdoors, enjoying the type of nature-centered experiences that she had as a child living in a more rural setting. After experimenting with a number of concepts, Kazakia settled on a simple but innovative product she called "Stick-Lets," pliable connectors that allow children to construct play structures (forts) using nothing more than a pile of twigs and tree branches (fig. 56).

Fig. 56
Christina Kazakia,
Stick-Lets, 2011

Human progress has historically been measured by our ability to rise above the influences of nature, and economic security by the rate at which natural resources could be transformed into utilitarian products. Today the danger of this mindset is plain. In *The Coming Transformation: Values to Sustain Human and Natural Communities*, former Dean of the Yale School of Forestry Gus Speth and social ecologist Stephen Kellert argue that environmental threats from global warming to decreased biodiversity cannot be solved through science, government, or economics alone. Rather, an optimistic future requires people being "truly convinced in their hearts and minds that the quality of our human existence depends on our ongoing experience and connection to a healthy natural world."[26] The Nature Lab provides just such a connection to the natural world, reminding us that our physical and emotional well-being is inextricably linked to our evolutionary heritage. Moreover, it emphasizes the critical role of artists and designers in exploring, interpreting, and representing nature's teachings to share values that embrace the living systems on Earth.

Notes

1. Stephen J. Gould, "Cabinet Museums: Alive, Alive, O!," in *Dinosaurs in a Haystack: Reflections in Natural History* (New York: Harmony Books, 1995), 244.

2. For further discussion on the future role of natural history museums in research and education see Kevin Winker, "Natural History Museums in a Postbiodiversity Era," *Bioscience* 54 (2004): 455–459.

3. E-mail to the author, December 14, 2012.

4. In the studio, students work from highly accurate reproductions of human skulls and skeletons. Real human skulls and skeletons are viewed through protective cases.

5. See http://museumtwo.blogspot.com/2010/05/guest-post-tale-of-two-university.html.

6. Julia Marshall, "Connecting Art, Learning, and Creativity: A Case for Curriculum Integration," *Studies in Art Education* 46 (2005): 227–241.

7. See Colleen J. Sheehy, *Cabinet of Curiosities: Mark Dion and the University as Installation* (Minneapolis: University of Minnesota Press, 2006), 128.

8. See http://www.art21.org/texts/mark-dion/interview-mark-dion-science-and-aesthetics.

9. See http://cjvrose.com/exhibit/stem-to-steam.

10. Archived papers of Edna Lawrence, Fleet Library, Rhode Island School of Design.

11. See http://oliviastreet.me/Biomimetics-in-Graphic-Design.

12. E-mail to the author, January 17, 2013.

13. See Vinodkumar Sarananthan et al., "Structure, Function, and Self-Assembly of Single Network Gyroid (I4132) Photonic Crystals in Butterfly Wing Scales," *Proceedings of the National Academy of Science* 107 (2010): 11,676–11,681; and Pete Vukusic and Ian Hooper, "Directionally Controlled Fluorescence Emission in Butterflies," *Science* 310 (2005): 1,151.

14. James H. Mathewson, "The Visual Core of Science: Definitions and Applications to Education," *International Journal of Science Education* 27 (2005): 529–548.

15. In conversation with the author, July 17, 2012.

16. Mengzhuo Li, Eliza Squibb, and Neal Overstrom, "Plankton Studio: Visual Inquiry and Imaging as Tools for Facilitating the Integration of Art and Science," *Abstracts from the 2012 EPSCoR Summer Undergraduate Research Fellows Conference*, July 27, 2012, University of Rhode Island, Kingston, RI, 101.

17. See James H. Mathewson, "Visual-Spatial Thinking: an Aspect of Science Overlooked by Educators," *Science Education* 83 (1999): 33–54.

18. See Maria Jose Pérez-Fabello and Alfredo Campos, "Influence of Training in Artistic Skills on Mental Imaging Capacity," *Creativity Research Journal* 19, nos. 2–3 (2007): 227–232.

19. Gerald Holton, "On the Art of the Scientific Imagination," *Daedalus* 125, no. 2 (1996): 183–208.

20. See Julia Marshall, "Connecting Art, Learning, and Creativity: A Case for Curriculum Integration," *Studies in Art Education* 46, no. 3 (2005): 227–341.

21. Peter K. Williamson, "The Creative Problem Solving Skills of Arts and Science Students—The Two Cultures Debate Revisited," *Thinking Skills and Creativity* 6, no. 1 (2011): 31–43.

22. For example, see Dutton's TED talk illustrated by animator Andrew Park at: http://www.ted.com/talks/denis_dutton_a_darwinian_theory_of_beauty.html, and his book, *The Art Instinct: Beauty, Pleasure and Human Evolution* (New York: Bloomberg Press, 2009). Also see a critique of Dutton's book by Mohan Matthen, "Art, Sexual Selection, Group Selection (Critical Notice of Denis Dutton, The Art Instinct)," *Canadian Journal of Philosophy* 41, no. 2 (2011): 337–356.

23. Roger S. Ulrich, "View Through a Window May Influence Recovery from Surgery," *Science* 224 (1984): 420–421.

24. Marc G. Berman, John Jonides, and Stephen Kaplan, "The Cognitive Benefits of Interacting with Nature," *Psychological Science* 19, no. 2 (2008): 1,207–1,212.

25. Richard Louv, *Last Child in the Woods: Saving Our Children from Nature-Deficit Disorder* (Chapel Hill, NC: Algonquin Books, 2005).

26. Stephen R. Kellert and James Gustave Speth, eds., *The Coming Transformation: Values to Sustain Human and Natural Communities* (Yale Printing and Publishing, 2009), 442.

Conversation: Critique

Eva Sutton

How can the ineffable, singular process of the critique—so vital
to art education and art making—be translated from the spoken
realm to the visual and back again? And what would we learn
from such a translation? Eva Sutton, Professor, Photography,
asked a group of five artists, designers, and faculty from the
RISD community (Christina Bertoni, Professor, Foundation
Studies; Daniel Hewett, Critic, Landscape Architecture; Norm
Paris, Assistant Professor, Foundation Studies; Elliott Romano,
BFA 2013 Photography; and Ian Stell, MFA 2012 Furniture
Design) to take up that challenge. Each created a visual
representation of their understanding of what happens during,
leading up to, and after the critique process, in an effort
to access the core function, effectiveness, and unique method-
ologies involved.

Art making follows an internal paradigm, an invisible metronome with inaudible rhythms. Design is a sympathetic resonance, an expressive response to something that calls for attention, but has yet to be fully understood or articulated. Although it is often perceived that artists, designers, and creative thinkers experience "eureka moments" in which a brilliant idea emerges, in practice, creativity is a long process. It often requires the maker to make something again and again, learning each time from the previous iteration.

The process of making has a solitary component, but it is immensely helpful to engage with others in a feedback loop, a conversation about the work in which the maker shows, speaks, sees, listens, and is listened to, a gathering of makers, each taking turns being on the spot, showing their work, and sharing the ideas behind it. This is the forum for understanding what was made and why. It is the conversation known as "critique." Critique is the space in which new work is shown, experiments are examined, and questions are asked. It is a time for honest observation, dispassionate listening, and plain talk. It is an incubator for ideas, a bubbling cauldron of opinion, and the place in which we make connections that we hadn't made before, moving toward understanding what it is we've made. At RISD, critique is the core of an art and design practice.

How do ideas flow in critique? What really happens in those studios full of art, design, and people? In response to these questions, six artists and designers gathered to talk about critique. Perhaps in a spirit of play, we decided to talk about a verbal form by returning to images. To begin, each participant made a drawing, or visual representation, of what the process of critique looks like to them. We didn't know what kinds of pictures would emerge, or if there would be any overlap; this was an experiment and we were curious to see the results.

The drawings show us that the flow from one idea to the next, the generation of new ideas from a conceptual core, and the dynamics of the conversation itself are processes that can be visualized. Each drawing is followed by the artist or designer's brief explanation, which is expanded on through

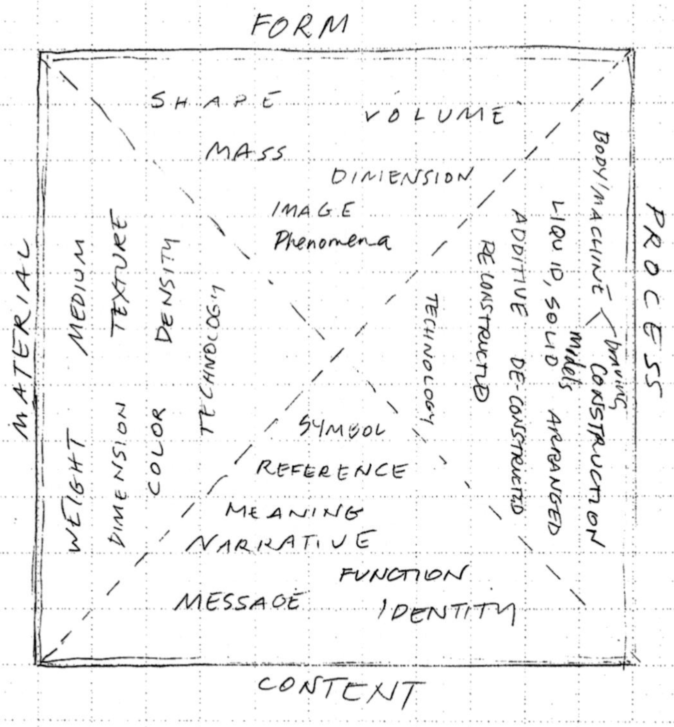

FORM

MATERIAL

PROCESS

SHAPE VOLUME
MASS
DIMENSION
IMAGE
Phenomena

MEDIUM
TEXTURE
DENSITY

WEIGHT
DIMENSION
COLOR
TECHNOLOGY

TECHNOLOGY

Body/Machine
Construction
moving
models
LIQUID, SOLID ARRANGED
ADDITIVE DE-CONSTRUCTED
RE-CONSTRUCTED

SYMBOL
REFERENCE
MEANING
NARRATIVE
MESSAGE FUNCTION
IDENTITY

CONTENT

the dialogue of the group. While the text often refers to the images, the intention is for the reader to interpret the descriptions of the critique process with regard to whichever medium he or she wishes. The word "image" is readily substituted with the word "object" in this sense, and that object could be real, existing in the physical space of the viewer, or virtual, manifested as data, network, or interface. In all cases, objects are experiences that can be shared and through which the maker speaks to the world.

Christina Bertoni, Professor, Foundation Studies

I give this diagram (fig. 57) to my students each year on the first day of my first-year Foundation class. It groups key terms and ideas into four major categories: form, content, material, and process. It's an organizing matrix that helps students to begin to identify fundamental aspects of thinking about their work and the work of their classmates. As much as they are practicing making in this class, they are also practicing how to talk about what they make and how to talk about what others have made. Offering students this matrix as a conceptual armature gives them confidence. It also sets reasonable boundaries for conversation during a critique.

EVA SUTTON These terms are all descriptive rather than judgmental, as some might expect given the term "critique."

CHRISTINE BERTONI Yes, it's useful for students to first describe what they're looking at, rather than decide whether or not they have an opinion of it. This forces them to put visuals into words, consider that relationship, and perhaps offer further connections. Under "form," for example, one could list words like "shape," "value," "mass," "dimension," "image," or "phenomena." Under "material," one might consider "weight," "texture," "color," "density," and "technology." These terms give students a framework from which to really start looking at things and understand what it is they're looking at. Judgment, at this stage, is beside the point. Also, if you talk about work in terms of coherence, the conversation can be more objective. Coherence is the synchronicity of form, material, content, and process. We have an innate recognition of coherence. If we can't find coherence in something, then we don't want to be bothered with it. So when I talk to students about coherence, it's about crafting an idea and using all the available structures selectively to support that idea and build on it. Alongside the notion of coherence, there's also meaning. In the matrix, I put "meaning" under "content." Meaning might be narrative. It might be referential. It might be language.

I think of critique as an articulation exercise, a way to get people to consider rather than judge. We've all had the experience of talking to a person about our work, especially if that person is not an artist, when suddenly, as we're talking, we say something that surprises us. Through the practice of talking about your work, you say things you didn't know you were aware of. It's important for students to know that talking out loud is another way of thinking, and that new thoughts come out through that process. Again, the matrix is simply a way to start this kind of conversation. Inevitably, a student will ask a question and break the conversation wide open, but the matrix gives students a framework so they can participate and not feel intimidated.

DANIEL HEWETT I appreciate your matrix in the same way I appreciate manners. The matrix allows students to come to the table and engage each other within a set of rules that negate neither personality nor position, and provide a level playing field for dialogue. You're giving them enough language to talk about the things they need to deal with, without giving so much language that you end up pinning them down.

NORM PARIS They're manners, but not in the Victorian sense; not a set of strict rules but rather guidelines that allow for a coherent community to develop among the participants.

DH Yes. As children, for instance, we learn manners as rules, but as we grow older, we learn to appreciate them as principles. I think this matrix does that as well.

Elliott Romano, BFA 2013 Photography

The process of making a new work and having it critiqued can be represented in a V-shaped, distillation diagram (fig. 58). You start with an idea and you make something based on it. In my experience, when the work is presented, one of the first things that often happens in the critique is that your peers start making connections between your work and other works. The questions that come up after that are often specific: "How was this piece made?" "What's it made of?" "What function does it have, or if it has a function, does it function properly?" "Is its function to somehow not function properly?" The interrogation expands to: "How does the piece fit into your general studio practice?" Finally, it comes back to the artist, who asks him- or herself, "Is this what I set out to do in the first place?" You have to examine how your finished work addresses your original concept, or whether it evolved completely into something else.

DH Is this an ideal thinking process for you, or is it a process you typically experience?

ELLIOTT ROMANO The drawing represents a streamlined ideal, but I always experience this same general movement downward, funneling into a converging end point. When a piece is being critiqued, I usually haven't had very much time yet to live with it or even to really just look at it. Sometimes, when I put a work up on the wall for critique, it's the first time I really see it. I have my perception of it, but it's when everyone else starts talking about it that I can reflect on what I think it is. During the conversation, I get feedback that either supports my assumption that the piece achieves what I set out to do, or it becomes clear that it hasn't, and that it's evolved into something else.

CB Sometimes when you're listening to this kind of conversation someone might make a suggestion that you know is a deal breaker. They're asking you to change something in the work that you can't give up, and that tells you something about what you really care about—it tells you where the heart of

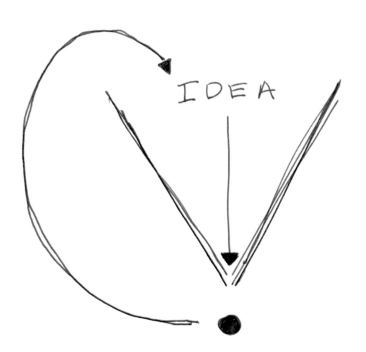

IDEA

your piece is. It's sometimes through those comments that you find that one thing without which the piece can't exist: the sine qua non.

DH You raise a great point about one of the most important distinctions students must make in the course of a critique. When challenged directly, how do we know when we're right or just being resistant? It can be really difficult to distinguish resistance to criticism from the perception that you're defending the essence of the work. When it feels like this is happening, stepping back from the work and just listening for the heart of the other's intended logic is often enough to reestablish a space for learning.

CB You need to hold the comments in your mind for a couple of days. Generally, in our life's work as artists, the same ideas come around again and again and you find that you're either coming back to an idea because you care about it or that you can be pried off of it pretty easily. It's only as we progress that we think, "I can't leave that idea alone, somehow."

ES It keeps popping up.

CB Compare a white pine to a sequoia. Some ideas pop up and reach maturity quickly while others just take forever to grow.

ES Elliott, you distinguish between being in the critique in the moment, simply letting thoughts come toward you, not putting up any barriers or defending yourself, and then later stepping back and having a private meditation on what was said.

Fig. 58
Elliott Romano,
critique diagram,
2013

CB As teachers, we need to urge our students to consider and to hang on to these comments and thoughts that emerge out of the critique, and either let them gather momentum or let them fade away.

NP That kind of reserving of judgment denotes a real maturity. I usually start off my semester with a quote by Robert Venturi about delaying judgment. To paraphrase, he says this delay makes further judgment more nuanced. I think it's absolutely necessary.

Norm Paris, Assistant Professor, Foundation Studies

This is an illustration of the various scenarios that can occur during a critique (fig. 59). In this building of some sort, the bottom level shows box molds with a cement mixer pouring something into a box. This illustrates a model I tend to avoid, the idea of a master teacher showing students how work is done. The next level shows an audio system emitting a signal that changes as it travels from speaker to audience. The next level is another iteration of that idea, illustrating what can happen in critiques when there are different factions of students, represented here as antennae, some gravitating toward each other's ideas, and others existing as polarities. Above that is a series of microphones, each with a satellite dish pointed toward culture at large, or the sounds that come from outside the domain of the classroom. Finally, the top level is a reconsideration of the cement-mixer model from the bottom level. Here, each student is his or her own cement mixer of ideas, pouring into the molds of others. It's a nonhierarchical model of dialogue.

CB Is there a relationship between the various levels?

NP Only in the sense that they are each distinct, except that the two speaker and antennae images are iterations of a similar concept. The top level is not intended to illustrate the highest form of critique. They're all about diagramming the social relationships within the critique, the kind of give-and-take that occurs.

CB Within this spectrum, where do you find yourself, in terms of engaging work or students?

Fig. 59
Norm Paris, critique diagram, 2013

NP As a Foundation Studies teacher, I'm caught between two places. I'm trying to teach a foundational level of approaches to making and drawing, but I'm also trying to nurture the specific ideas of the students. So for me, the balance is in working with the student to find his or her own way through a given project, while also ensuring the student gains a level of understanding about formal drawing ideas. I don't subscribe to just one model.

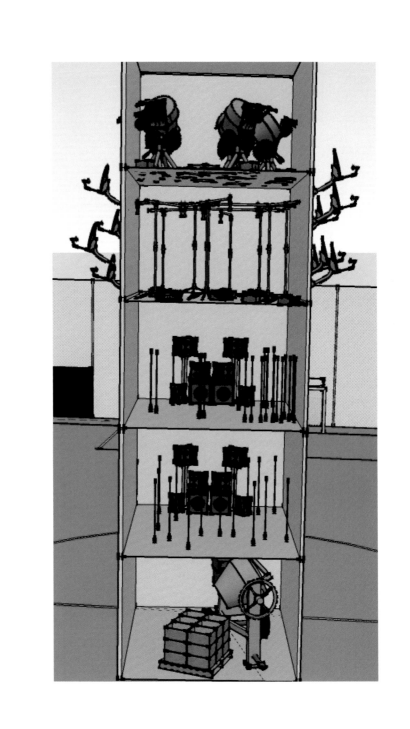

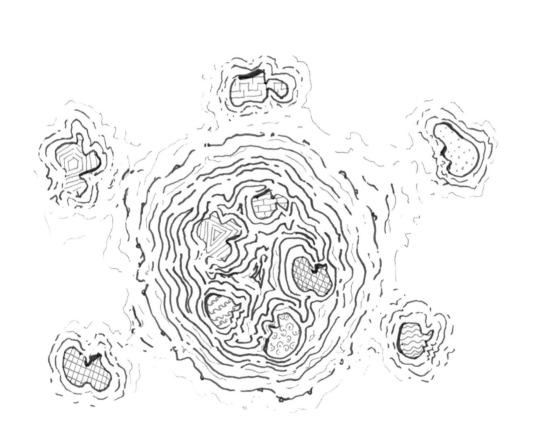

CB What makes a model of critique effective?

NP It's knowing how to hear what the students "remixed" for me and for their fellow students. It's knowing when to control a discussion but also when to let the discussion find its own terrain. That makes for effective facilitation. But this whole structure could exist in a fenced-off field somewhere. To that point, all these ideas are part of an internal dialogue within an institution that itself has boundaries. It's important to consider those boundaries, to at times stay within them, and at times push beyond them. When I'm teaching drawing, I'm often communicating ideas that come from a traditional Western perspective. It's important to acknowledge the specificity of those ideas and the fact that they're not the only ideas.

Ian Stell, MFA 2012 Furniture Design
I see the process of critique as an amoeba-like organism, or a concurrence of threads—a unique process for each participant that is never the same twice (fig. 60). It is as much an accumulation as it is a linear progression toward a single truth or idea. It can be described as a maze, a knot, respiration, or a tidal cycle. The roles of student and teacher are fluid, and everyone stands to both learn and to instruct in an open critique.

My diagram could be interpreted in a number of ways. Basically, there are five satellite forms around a central body. Each of these outer forms has a corresponding twin in the center (a matching shape), but the satellites and the shapes in the center are composed of different patterns. The differing patterns suggest a recognizable, empathic connection, but also indicate that the forms are not identical copies. This represents a resonance, which could also be seen as an interpretation or a focused emphasis.

Fig. 60
Ian Stell, critique
diagram, 2013

DH Do you have an intention about the direction of movement in the drawing?

IAN STELL No, I don't. The movement goes in both directions and is very fluid.

DH One thing that I take from this drawing is how intuitively we do these things. We've done critique a lot, but it's still really difficult to explain what it is, even if you know how to represent it. It's highly intuitive, and so it is difficult to put words to your image, but the image feels authentic.

ES I like the fact that it looks so biological. It looks like it could be something cellular, and there's a kind of a dynamism to it that represents what you want a critique to be.

CB Yes, you captured that sense of a critique as a pulsing field of energy. Everybody's radar is on. Their antennae are vibrating. They're picking up signals and often you don't know whether they're being ingested by ideas or separating from them.

IS One thing that came to mind when I started drawing this is that it was both a permeable entity that's breathing and allowing things to pass through it, and also a maze. Getting from the outside to the inside requires trial and error, analysis, and effort.

ES Can you elaborate on the effort involved in getting inside the maze, and what might happen if one gets lost?

IS It's interesting that you used the word "lost." The maze has no clear conclusion. I don't want to imply that you can miss the center or that there's a wrong answer or a wrong place to be, but instead emphasize that the maze requires you to really engage with it, through discrimination and focus.

The outer shapes can represent individual voices responding to a particular student or body of work in the center, but they can also be seen as the converse: individual students being responded to by a group. The reversibility of these components conveys the fluctuating sense among the participants that sometimes they're on the inside and sometimes on the outside.

CB Say you do get trapped in a maze, you have to turn around and go back to get to the main road and find your way again. When you're working on an idea and it seems like you've reached a dead end, you should go back to your sources and you may be able to approach the problem again in a better way.

NP I'm wondering if you always have to go back to the main road, or if the maze is an infinitely reconstructible thing, so that if you're at a dead end, you can actually move a wall and get back to the main road more directly.

ES The idea of being able to move a wall indicates a kind of reframing. So the maze is your understanding of a process, and if you move a wall, so to speak, you've reframed the problem.

IS Exactly. The image evokes an undetermined kind of space. That's one of the central interests I have in critique. The maker could be speaking about something that is concrete to a certain degree and may be materially defined, but the way it's understood and perceived is all in flux around it.

ER When I look at the drawing, I see the rings of a tree, a kind of natural maze. It looks like something that's continuously growing. So you have your central idea, which you can follow outward; you're constantly moving and the idea is constantly growing.

Daniel Hewett, Critic, Landscape Architecture

In creating this representation, I thought about the meeting of different experiences and perspectives—the critique for me, a teacher, and the critique as it is experienced by a student (fig. 61). I drew a square in the middle of a large piece of paper. My experience is that a student will often come to a critique with a solid sense of what the work is about: that's the square. What I pay attention to is not the square, but everything around it. For instance, the other things they mention, the way they behave, their learning style, and my sense of how much they can actually learn within the scope of this moment, project, or semester. The result is a conversation about something bigger than the original square.

I often tell students that I'm not actually interested in their work itself. What I'm interested in is the work as a vehicle for understanding their potential to learn. It's not as much about making "good" work as it is about making work that creates opportunities for the little bit you're capable of learning on the project and just leaving out the rest. Out of this will often come a conversation that includes more than just what they brought me. I'm looking for the thing they're not saying or seeing that may be limiting their understanding.

If all goes well, this dialogue generates a kind of clarity about the making process, represented here by the crease I've made in the paper. The goal is to come out of it with some idea or conceptual structure that, because it is clearly defined and precise, is an order that we can build on or bounce off. It can align our thoughts long enough for us to move our understanding forward in a coherent way. Locating coherence is highly intuitive and can come from many different places. Because it is about everything outside the original square, it is mostly about listening for long enough to hear something operative and essential.

CB He gets 10 points for describing critique three-dimensionally.

IS Can you talk a little bit about time in relation to this process?

DH It depends on the complexity of a project. If it were a one-day exercise the frame of the discussion would have to be scaled in such a way that the learning can happen. But there are other times when the process can expand and take the whole semester or more.

Fig. 61
Daniel Hewett,
critique diagram, 2013

IS I respect what you say about not being as interested in the work itself but in the learning that comes from it. That's key because often the epiphany, or that perfect crease or fold, almost never happens within the actual time-frame of the project or the semester.

ES I think that, ultimately, you can't teach anyone anything. Students have to come up with it themselves. I feel total resonance with the idea of the teacher becoming invisible and letting the ideas emerge from the maker.

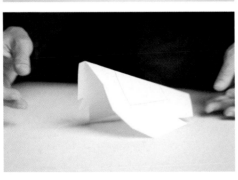

random ideas

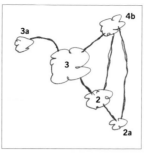

sprouts emerge

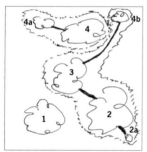

loosely connected ideas

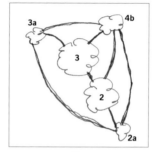

connections grow

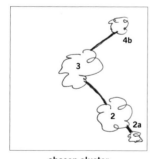

clusters of related ideas

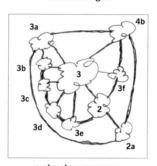

a structure emerges

chosen cluster

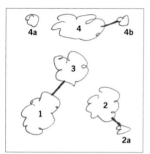

the core idea becomes clear

CB And that's a very tricky thing to do because you have to make sure you're nurturing your students actively, but then you have to decide when they're ready for you to step back further and further, to the point where you do become invisible.

ER In certain critiques there comes a point in which the room becomes silent and it allows for whoever is being critiqued to become introspective. It's almost like a forced meditation; you're left with these really condensed ideas and that's where the breakthrough can come.

Eva Sutton, Professor, Photography

My diagram is about the formation of ideas as the conversation of critique evolves over time (fig. 62). As you have ongoing critique conversations, week after week, ideas are revealed—like a group of clouds, numbered in the drawing, that are not yet connected. As these ideas are presented, the conversation among their author and others guide the ideas into loose proximity. We start to get some lines of connectivity between these idea clouds, and as the conversation evolves each week, the lines become more structured.

Then we begin to see a clustering of similar ideas that relate more closely to one another and cause some clouds to come together and separate from each other simultaneously. This represents a realization of connections as well as distinctions between ideas. This process of convergence and divergence makes the ideas clearer to the maker. Choices are made as to which ideas are kept and which are discarded (for now) in a "pruning" process. From the kept ideas, sprouts emerge. The structure is refined. It develops multiple, stronger connections. A central core emerges: the generative idea.

Now we have increased clarity, a more refined, crystalline structure branching from this core idea, which I labeled as "3," an arbitrary number. It is the generative idea that has been discovered, that the structure both points to and emanates from, and that the maker now understands. From this generative idea, a considered body of work can emerge. The idea became

Fig. 62
Eva Sutton, critique
diagram, 2013

clear during the iterative conversations between the maker and the group, and it serves as a reference point from which to anchor new work in support of it.

NP During a critique, ideas are viral among participants—they mingle, and the influence of that mingling is really dynamic. The benefit of influence in a group dialogue is huge. That crystallization is wonderfully evasive and allows for many different curves and changes along the maker's way.

DH It's like an interpretive dance, moving somehow toward a kind of intention, toward an emerging synchrony.

ES The critique process is meandering, following a line that varies in both width and direction. The energy of the process lies in that variation. The maker offers his or her work to the group and the group responds. A conversation ensues. The real meaning of the work emerges when the intention of its maker, as expressed in words, and the responses from its audience begin to converge. Although the systems of words and images are asymptotic and may never actually merge, they can approach each other closely. The closer the convergence, the clearer the meaning of the work. The work communicates as intended—at least in part.

Spoken language, as a system of expression, is both constrained and vast. Images, too, involve rules and constraints, but also provide limitless possibilities. The translation from images into words and back again is an inexact mapping. Like the gap between neural synapses, this open connection is a conduit for thought. At times, images and words are in sync, reinforcing each other. Other times, they are at odds. Throughout the critique process, it is important to acknowledge the limitations of language. Images and objects are, after all, articulations of the unspoken. Too many words can flatten the complexity of expression or rob it of its mystery. An elusive quality should be allowed to inhabit the work, unspeakable, but at the same time perceivable and palpable. But all correlations and contradictions are worth examining. When do the responses from an audience, put to words, match one's own perception of the image, or object, being considered? When do they contradict? The tension and synergy between the two systems offer a way forward: a progressive spiral between thinking/making and speaking/listening. It is the repetition of these actions that make up critique—the process by which the work and our understanding of its meaning evolve.

Acting into the Unknown

Pradeep Sharma

How do external partners benefit from collaboration with
RISD? And what has RISD learned in the process of such
collaboration? Pradeep Sharma, Dean of Architecture
and Design, describes how improvisation, process, guessing,
uncertainty, practice, and failure all play into the meaningful
development of creativity and innovation. In the end,
RISD partnerships, while committed to sharing special
skills, expertise, and strategies, are largely about cultivating
the opportunity and freedom to enter the unknown.

I remember as a consultant being asked to help a company with innovation. Their opening salvo: "We tried design once. It didn't work." This was many years ago, and since then plenty has been written about the role of design in business. Today, of course, design is everywhere. We all recognize that design plays a significant role not just in products and services but also in brand positioning, loyalty, productivity, and organizational structures. Yet all this attention hardly clarifies what we mean when we speak of design. The broad definitions end up being too general to pin it down, while the specific ones exclude too much. Today's trendiest books and articles teach us about design management or design methods or design thinking. Yet designing is as old as civilization; we've been doing it ever since we purposefully set out to make something.

Given all this loose talk, the design community would do well to take a page from the quality movement of the last century. One of the best things that movement did was to ban the word "quality" so that we needed to define exactly what we meant when we reached for the word. Likewise, if we are to make sense of design strategy and innovation in an organization, we might well ban the word "design" so as to pay closer attention to what we actually find ourselves doing, often in collaboration with other people, when we seek solutions to problems. Sometimes definitions are artificial and problematic. Still, they help us locate ourselves, and our thinking. They provide us a shared compass.

When we speak of design, we also typically speak of "creativity" and "innovation"—two terms that are often used interchangeably but that are also open to many different interpretations. Here, I will propose creativity as a behavior and innovation as a process. Creativity as a behavior is something that we can bring to anything that we do—it implies both thought and act. By contrast, innovation is a social process. To try to clarify that process, we can look at invention, innovation, and entrepreneurship as a series of activities. Let's say we make something new. Just because we've invented something doesn't mean that anyone is using it. Using that new something is a socializing process in which we must present the invention to other people, then convince them to use it. That's innovation. So now we've invented something new and convinced people to use it; we still haven't established that we're making any money. That's entrepreneurship. And where is creativity in all this? Present throughout. Quite simply, creativity is the behavior that animates the innovation process.

If this description of invention, innovation, and entrepreneurship seems to imply a serial process, it is not meant to; the purpose of this separation is to highlight two key points. First, various behaviors inform each process—behaviors like divergent thinking and convergent thinking, giving form to ideas, prototyping, and testing. Second, the same person may not be appropriate for each process. We can establish a business, for example, without necessarily being the inventor. And thus we need to collaborate.

Recognizing the creative links from invention to innovation to entrepreneurship and the vital nature of collaboration, Rhode Island School of Design fosters many engagements with industry. Indeed, we actively explore innovation processes in business in five key forms: Partnered Studios, Innovation Studios, Workshops, Salons, and Fellowships. These take place in the context of art and design, and they are based in a single discipline or multiple disciplines. In every case, they actively engage in an exploration of creativity and innovation.

Fig. 63
"Design for Extreme Environments: Common Crew Cabin," with NASA, 2011

In Partnered Studios, a sponsoring company works collaboratively with partners at RISD to develop an area of inquiry that is simultaneously of interest to the company and of academic benefit to the student and faculty participants (figs. 63 and 64). Participants then work alone and in groups to invent concepts and prototypes, which they present to the community for critique. The critique is an essential part of the process: It encourages the community of inquirers—the sponsoring company, studio participants, and invited critics—to interrogate the design. The aim is to make things better. Applying the rules

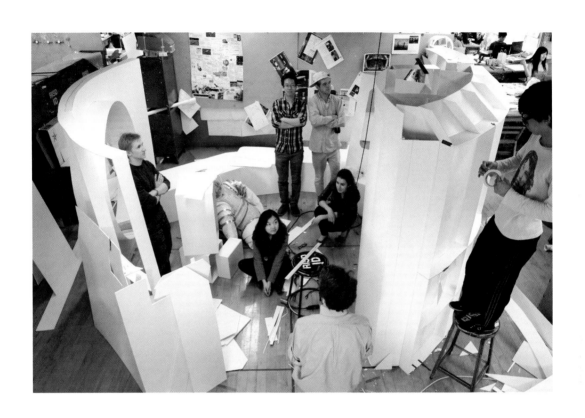

of good improvisation, each critic tries to avoid painting other members into a corner, while presenting opportunities to build on everyone's ideas. This iterative process emphasizes reflection and reflexivity for the individual and for the group, generating multiple perspectives that inform the group's collective understanding of the problem space and of possible solutions.

The Innovation Studio requires active collaboration from the start. There is still a community of inquirers and there are still critiques, but the problems, sometimes called *wicked problems*, tend to be much more complex, often contradictory and paradoxical. This process requires a lot more facilitation and guidance. The role of the facilitator is to act not only as project manager, intermediary, and sometimes peacemaker, but also as someone who maintains the sanity of the group—which can expect to experience both power dynamics and emotional pressure. Innovation Studios provoke a psychosocial process, bringing together real people with differing experiences and expectations and real lives. Like wicked problems, they become journeys of not only discoveries of problems, but also of the self.

Workshops are similar to Innovation Studios but are of shorter duration and often focus on a particular topic or access to skills. They include external invited guest participants and typically last two to five days. Participants spend the first day presenting information, then work in groups to develop techniques or solutions. Investigative processes, problem-solving approaches, critical making, and critique are ever-present. Salons are shorter than workshops, seldom lasting longer than a day, and include more open-ended dialogue. They tend to be about sharing ideas; presenters may be asked to share their thoughts or methods and then others question and help develop content. The aim of a Salon is to stretch the way we look at things.

Fellowships are programs in which a company sends one or more of its executives to be immersed in the RISD experience. These executives come for whole semesters, take part in classes, and make work with advisors who both coach and tutor them in ways that support their journeys with creativity and expression. The key to this approach is to ensure that the

Fig. 64
"The Green Studio,"
with Kimberly-Clark,
2010

visiting executives are really here and present in the moment, physically and mentally. The advisor helps them choose courses and provides contextual links from a variety of educational experiences and departments. The overall aim is to encourage applying the resourcefulness and adaptability of design approaches to all problem solving and to foster greater self-awareness through visual thinking.

Each of these formats suits the particular aims of the interaction; longer partnered projects are aimed at developmental research and shorter salons are aimed at executive education. Although the formats might seem common to learning environments, what is new is how broadly RISD applies them to business, research, and global concerns. So what have we learned over the years in working with small, medium, and large, local and multinational companies?

1. Beware generalization.

The saying in research is that we discover what we see—that is, our already present attitudes and dispositions influence our sense-making. As designers and artists we try to hold on to complexity and ambiguity for a little bit longer, to not clarify too early. Learning from particular examples—with their particular people and their particular contexts—we try to avoid the tendency to form generalizations, which can become limiting, especially as they evolve into rules for "what one must do." In other words, we are careful about how we particularize the generalizations of the particularizations—if that makes sense. Artists are especially good at living with paradoxes and uncertainty. Rather than trying to reduce situations and dissect them, they tend to *make something* that explains the phenomenon to themselves. This is exactly the kind of habit that, say, policy-makers would do well to develop.

2. Attention coexists with intention.

Process is fundamental to designing. We use process sometimes as a method, sometimes as a philosophical approach. Designers employ process as an act of improvisation rather than as a fully predetermined path, favoring attention over intention and thinking about how we proceed from one phenomenon to the next. Lane Myer, Senior Critic in the Furniture Design and Sculpture departments at RISD, proposes that the notion of proceeding gets us to think about what we have to do to move past things, to get around things.[1] In a sense, *proceeding* has neither a speed nor a direction. Sometimes to proceed we may have to go backward. Process is not smooth, but a staccato pattern of leaps. When we pay attention to our process, we start to see each staccato leap more clearly—how some points are actually problems, while others help us move ahead.

Process should not be confused with strategy. In management terms "strategy" is used to direct action in an organization. It implies that we have the ability to visualize a preferred future and plot a path toward it. The reality— "the process"—is much messier. The etymology of "process" highlights a course of action, "many smaller strategies." It incorporates and thrives on shifting and varied roles, technologies, skills, and resources, and on the influences of everyday things such as politics, culture, power negotiations, acts of interpretation, and expressions of emotion.

How easy it is to be seduced by the notion that implementation is smooth, linear, and rational. For earlier generations, in a time of mass industrialization and rigid hierarchies, the notion of direct causal relationships between action and effect may have held up. More recently, though, chaos theory and the complexity sciences have challenged that notion and introduced the idea that phenomena are not necessarily directly related and can result in unpredictable outcomes. Recognizing this nonlinearity, through process, better serves people working in today's complex, fast-moving, networked, hyper-competitive fields. Sure, we may still dream of a "smooth process." When we look back at the actions we've enacted, we package them in a coherent narrative, a simple synoptic that tells a smooth, logical story. But the reality is always different, especially when we confront today's most compelling problems, and especially when we're looking forward. In fact, it is at the beginning of the process—the fuzzy front end when we don't really know what the problem is and what we want to do—that process is most essential.

3. Guessing is a valid form of logic.

Today's organizations are populated largely by people educated in analytical disciplines. This is certainly true of those who studied quantitative subjects, but it's also true in the liberal arts. Two means of inference have traditionally influenced these disciplines: inductive reasoning (bottom-up logic, reaching a conclusion from specific examples) and deductive reasoning (top-down logic, reaching a conclusion from a general premise). Like strategy, each of these forms of reasoning presents a clear, smooth, logical path to a solution.

But there's still another kind of logic that has recently gained currency in business and organizational-learning circles.[2] Charles Sanders Peirce, the American pragmatist philosopher of a century ago, suggested an alternative means of inference: abductive reasoning.[3] Abductive reasoning assigns special status to guessing as an efficient, sufficient mode of logic. For example, you know that Jack and Jill recently had a row that ended their friendship, but then you see them jogging together. You conclude that the best explanation is that they are friends again. Your hypothesis supports your conclusion, but it doesn't necessarily prove the conclusion. Most philosophers agree that abduction is frequently employed and essential to our everyday practice, even if its normative status is still a matter of controversy. (The skeptical view is that we apply abductive reasoning so frequently that it may become too automatic.)

We jump to abductive inferences all the time in design processes, as a way to proceed. As Buckminster Fuller once suggested, sometimes positive things happen inadvertently when we proceed "precessionally"—at 90 degrees to where we are heading:

The honeybees are chromosomically programmed to enter the flower blossoms in search of honey. Seemingly inadvertently (but realisticallyprecessionally) this occasions the bees' bumbling tails becoming dusted with pollen (at 90 degrees to each bee's linear axis and flight path), whereafter the bees further bumbling entries into other flowers inadvertently dusts off, pollinizes, and cross-fertilizes at right angles (precessionally) to the bees' operational axis.

Bees make flowers bloom with their inadvertent bumbling, and so might humans pollinate new possibilities with their guessing. At the same time, Fuller injects a subtle warning about always following the bees: "Humans, as honey-money-seeking bees, do many of nature's required tasks only inadvertently."[4] Indeed, in addition to guessing, we also reflect, review, and revise.

4. Expect uncertainty.

Mechanistic models of organizational change are dominated by assumptions of stability, routine, and order, in which we move from one static situation to another. Kurt Lewin, the founder of social psychology, characterized this model as "unfreezing-moving-freezing."[5] This sort of organizational change was reified in the twentieth century, when in fact organic models are more appropriate for the changing environments of today, and even of the past. In the fourth century BCE, Heraclitus said, "No man ever steps in the same river twice, for it's not the same river and he's not the same man." Why should we believe 25 centuries later that anything is different? When I talk to managers and ask them what an average day looks like, they always say that no two days are the same. There is always change.

Another model that has been questioned in recent years is rational-choice theory: the idea that we will make sensible, rational choices, weighing up the pros and cons and acting accordingly. The problem, of course, is that people are not rational. As behavioral economist Dan Ariely suggests, we are instead "predictably irrational."[6] Even in organizations whose authorities have indoctrinated people to think the same and act from a script, those authorities cannot possibly take into account every circumstance and every scenario and hence determine behavior. And not all organizations are the same. They are made up of a unique collection of people, histories, and circumstances, so we should not make the mistake of assuming that something that worked in one organization will work in the same way in another. The patterns of organizing, behavior, sense-making, and interrelating in each organization will always be diverse.

Psycho-sociological issues add additional complications to any intellectual model we might try to apply. As soon as two people get together, culture and interrelationships develop and over time become somewhat habitual. But that doesn't mean that relationships are predictable. People arrive at any encounter with differing needs. It is very rare that we all agree on everything. Sometimes we behave in ways that are determined by something happening somewhere else in our life, introducing unforeseen conflicts. Indeed, Michel Foucault argues that conflict, not conformity, is the norm in all relationships.[7] He also challenges the idea that power is wielded by people or groups by way of "episodic" or "sovereign" acts of domination or coercion, seeing power instead as dispersed, pervasive, enabling, constraining, and in a constant state of flux.

The physical sciences have made significant advances over the centuries, especially with regard to mathematical modeling of phenomena and our ability to predict from it. Seduced by this way of thinking, we have developed the view that we can model not only physical phenomena but also social phenomena, that humans are autonomous individuals who behave rationally and whose behavior can be modeled to make predictions. Nobel Laureate Ilya Prigogine, following many decades of classical scientific thought, contended that such determinism is no longer viable in science. Predictions are even less reliable in social interactions: Human behavior is too pluralistic.

5. Communicate toward joint action.

Together, all of these revised intellectual models challenge the mechanistic thinking that organizations and people will do as management dictates. So how can we move forward in such a state of unpredictability? In design, design thinking, and creativity, the context matters, but so do the individuals who take part. Paradoxically, we have to make sense of the organization's requirements and each person's needs at the same time. We are all socialized, of course, but when it comes to trying to do something specific together, we must find a way to articulate joint action, to develop a language for what it is that we want to do. In all of our collaborative work at RISD, we spend a lot of time developing a collective language, which starts with forming a common sense of "us." This is not as easy as it sounds. Groups are by nature full of plural identities and plural aspirations. Thus, there are methods for joint action: actions and ideas have to be justified; people have to convince and be convinced. With advances in communication technologies, we sometimes forget the importance of the little gestures that communicate much more than words. Embodied dialogue is also very much a part of the collaborative process.

6. Practice, practice, practice.

Designing, painting, and managing are all *practices*, which implies two things: first, that we have to do something in order to understand it; and second, that we get better the more we do it. In other words, to be a good practitioner requires both practice and experience. For John Dewey experience was at the root of all learning: "Every experience should do something to prepare a person for later experiences of a deeper and more expansive quality," he wrote. "That is the very meaning of growth, continuity, reconstruction of experience."[8] Aristotle described *phronesis* (practical wisdom) as innate to us, unlike *episteme* (theoretical knowledge) and *techne* (skill), which can be learned and forgotten. Still, all three require practice.

7. Don't be afraid to fail/be afraid to fail.

Lane Myer describes a drawing exercise he assigns to demonstrate how the mind and hand collaborate to perform a task, yet how the mind always blames the hand for any resulting mishap. He asks participants to place a dot exactly in the center of an empty sheet of white paper. This is not as easy as it sounds. Upon failing, most people quickly become self critics, bemoaning that their hand was "off" in missing the center. The exercise and resulting response—the mind seeing the hand's work as "wrong"—suggests why so few people draw after childhood.

It's become almost axiomatic that designers are unafraid to fail. But I challenge that notion. *We should be afraid to fail.* Fear of failure is an essential part of being human, whether it manifests as anxiety about an unknown future, performance anxiety, social anxiety, or existential anxiety. Such anxieties are supremely difficult to endure, but if we are going to change, anxiety must be present. *Creative* anxiety is necessary for reflexivity, and is even, I would argue, an expression of freedom. We should be afraid to fail, but do it anyway.

By now it should be clear that creativity is not exclusive to art and design; it is a fundamental human action. Yet for a simple process that we have been successfully accomplishing for countless millennia, creativity remains extremely complex, even contradictory. We might think, for example, that creativity is exclusive and inclusive, or individual and social. It is typical to regard contradictions as dichotomous: as polarized oppositions requiring an "either/or" choice—as in "theory and practice," which we artificially separate, even though one continually informs the other. We might also regard contradiction as a dilemma: a choice between two equally unattractive alternatives. Alternatively, we could see a contradiction as a duality: a "both/and" way of thinking, a paradox—a state in which two diametrically opposing forces or ideas are simultaneously present; neither can be resolved or eliminated. Holding on to paradox may help us be more innovative in our practice as we recall that paradoxes exist not only "out there" but also within us.

Innovation requires thinking and doing at the same time about things we haven't imagined yet. The challenge is to not treat the contradictions or paradoxes as barriers but as foundations for discourse—and, hopefully, action. The creative process is by no means deterministic and certain; but neither is it random. As art and design educators, we work hard with our students, ourselves, and our collaborators to pay attention, act accordingly, and to constantly challenge our thinking. Doing so requires creating a culture that accepts open confrontation. It is not easy, for we are challenging what's most fundamental: who we are as people, with all the experiences that have made us and our apparent knowledge. To change, we must at some stage understand something differently. Collaborating toward innovation is really about acting into the unknown. When does it all make sense? Only once we do something.

Notes

1. Interview with the author, March 7, 2013.

2. See, for example, Roger Martin, *The Design of Business: Why Design Thinking Is the Next Competitive Advantage* (Boston: Harvard Business School Publishing, 2009), 64–67.

3. See Charles Sanders Peirce, "Guessing," in *The Hound and the Horn* (April–June 1929): 267–282.

4. R. Buckminster Fuller, *Critical Path* (New York: St. Martin's Press, 1981), 141.

5. Kurt Lewin, *Field Theory in Social Science* (New York: Harper & Row, 1951).

6. Dan Ariely, *Predictably Irrational: The Hidden Forces That Shape Our Decisions* (New York: HarperCollins, 2008).

7. Michel Foucault, *Power/Knowledge* (New York: Pantheon Books, 1980).

8. John Dewey, *Experience & Education* (New York: Simon & Schuster, 1997), 47.

Afterword

Mara L. Hermano

I am not a maker. Not in the sense that my colleagues and the young people around me are makers—using their hands as extensions of their minds to construct objects that communicate ideas and engage aesthetic sensibilities. But there are some similarities between my work and theirs. I work together with these makers to determine what RISD has accomplished in the past, to discern where we are now, in our own context as well as those of higher education and the world at large, and to articulate and realize a vision for the future. Because I was trained as an art historian, the most basic and most valuable tool in my kit is observation. I feel privileged to observe students and faculty in process at RISD. I get to look at, smell, and, yes, touch the artwork here. I get to observe objects being made. And just as I get to observe objects in process, I get to see young artists and designers in process too—just as they are making, they are also being made (see fig. 65).

This book provides a provocative and thoughtful glimpse into a RISD education. The faculty and staff contributors reveal pedagogies developed over time, detailing assignments, prompts, and projects; sharing examples of student, faculty, and alumni work; and surveying pedagogical modes of delivering unique training in art and design. This is a demonstration of not only how to make art and design, but also how to make artists and designers. More than a compendium of tools and strategies, this book is a reflection of the distinctive environment at RISD, which Naomi Mishkin (BFA 2012 Glass) notes, "isn't a group of buildings, a faculty list, or a facilities list. It's about taking the most driven, impassioned, talented, insane, outspoken, brilliant, curious insomniacs, putting them in the same room, and letting them run wild doing exactly what they want to do. RISD is people, place, and common questions."[1]

When we consider the core concept of "critical making" at RISD, we acknowledge there is no single formula for it. Critical making depends on a host of factors, influences, and methodologies, but relies chiefly on four basic elements: process, context, material knowledge, and questioning. Students arrive at RISD ready to work, and to work hard. They are impatient

to start in on process, and approach their first studio courses with serious intentions. Regardless of their area of study, students will make more things than they have ever made before, using processes they didn't even know existed. As Elizabeth Kripke, a fourth-year student in the Brown-RISD Dual Degree program studying painting and neuroscience points out, "The fact that RISD students are constantly making is what sets this style of education apart from more traditional academic experiences. Creative making, which inherently necessitates invention, means one must face the edge of known experience, and push beyond it."[2]

To address the diversity of context required for critical making, the RISD community offers up its abundant collections and programs. The RISD Museum encourages engagement and dialogue with objects across history; the artifacts and specimens in the Edna Lawrence Nature Lab promote knowledge of nature and natural systems while supporting artists and designers in the exploration, interpretation, and representation of living systems; and the liberal arts courses, in the words of Daniel Cavicchi, Dean of Liberal Arts, in this volume, "emphasize not only disciplinary education but also the development of critical makers who are ethical, critical, and articulate, and are wide-ranging enough to provide an exciting new set of 'possibles'…at their core, liberal and studio arts are both processes of making."

The fundamental nature of material knowledge to critical making can be summed up in a statement made by Kelly Dobson, Professor, Digital+Media, in the chapter "Conversation: Materials," in which she engages several RISD professors in conversation about their relationships with materials in their practice: "Materials and forces are the basis of making. We apply pressure and imagination to materials and they become meaningful to us." Within this framework of process, context, and material knowledge, questions must continually be asked, such as those set forth by students Carly Ayres (BFA 2013 Industrial Design) and Sarah Pease (BFA 2013 Furniture Design) in their practice: "Does this thing need to exist? What problem is it solving? Will this product have a negative impact on the world?"[3]

Fig. 65
Jude Landry,
"Makers Gonna Make"
temporary tattoo

Despite how embedded and focused the process of critical making is, RISD does not operate in a vacuum. Higher education is experiencing an unprecedented moment of change. Technology, economics, globalization, the environment, and demographics have a direct impact on the curriculum and the future of higher education. The clarity and direct nature of RISD's mission will ensure its viability in years to come; making is what happens here and it is what we do best. But we must also recognize the world our students enter when they leave. At a time when unemployment rates are high, institutions of higher education are being called on to certify that students have the knowledge and skills to become productive citizens. Sociologist Steven J. Tepper notes, concerning careers for arts alumni, that "we have moved from an 'Elf' to a 'Fairy' economy—from predictable, organizationally based, well-defined division of labor to an economy where people are highly mobile, working for whomever needs them, doing whatever job is necessary, and bringing to the table broad and diverse skills."[4] The nature of a career itself is changing, and the new versatility—a mobile system requiring diversity and creativity—may place arts alumni in a position of advantage. President John Maeda has often said that because of their RISD experience our students have the capacity to thrive in a volatile, uncertain, complex, and ambiguous (VUCA) world.[5] At RISD, we are not just preparing students for a world that is rapidly changing, we are preparing students to change the world by their own making and remaking of it. We are bringing forth critical makers— artists and designers who can propose answers for the future by continually asking new questions in the present.

Because critical making focuses on questioning, students learn to operate under a high level of uncertainty. This enables them to cope with criticism, cooperate with others who have differing opinions and perspectives, and prepare for an unpredictable world. Mishkin reflects, "As artists, we commit ourselves to being lifelong learners. We live in uncertainty and constant flux." Likewise, Kripke's interdisciplinary experience leads her to observe that "scientists, parallel to physical makers, are constantly at the edge of established knowledge, attempting to push beyond it to establish new theories and ultimately, knowledge. This process of discovery, common to both fine art and research science, is what I am excited to explore as I leave RISD."

As institutions of higher education, philanthropic foundations, and other scholarly organizations engage in defining the most significant learning outcomes for students in the twenty-first century, critical and creative thinking have consistently emerged on top. Like these skills, critical making demands curiosity, questioning, and listening; uniquely, it also demands eagerness to observe, to examine a problem from all sides, to test assumptions, to make and remake prototypes again and again, to thrive and evolve in the environment of critique, and to think and make always (see fig. 65). In an unpredictable world, RISD graduates are adaptive and flexible because they are accustomed to questioning, responding, making, and remaking both their environments and objects of their own invention. The critical makers who emerge from RISD leave not fully formed, but with minds and hands primed to ask questions, ready to look ahead to the next problem and to find new solutions. A common art-historical question asks, "How does an artist know when a work of art is finished?" At RISD, we might also inquire, "How do we know when a maker has been made?" One answer to the first question is that a work of art is never finished, as long as it continues to produce new responses. The answer to the second question is that a maker is never finished being made, because the making always continues.

Notes

1. Conversation with the author, April 2, 2013.

2. Conversation with the author, March 31, 2013.

3. Conversation with the author, March 28, 2013.

4. Steven J. Tepper, "Welcome Address," Strategic National Arts Alumni Project Conference, Nashville, TN, March 2013.

5. The use of the VUCA acronym in this context is from Dr. Bob Johansen, Distinguished Fellow, Institute for the Future, address to the American Council on Education National Conference, Washington, DC, March 2011.

Acknowledgments

At RISD the range of creative practice, teaching, and learning is vast and complex. Our thanks go to all the contributors in this book who worked to capture what is both definitive and abstract about the process of art and design education, particularly around creative disciplines and modes of learning. Each contributor expressed a reflective understanding fortified with clear expertise. The results will invite a broad group of readers to gain perspective on what happens in our classrooms and studios, and even on how that translates into life after RISD in the professional lives of our alumni as successful practitioners. Thanks to each of the authors for their commitment to this project and to the messages that form a common yet wonderfully textured and varied educational vision.

It would be inconceivable to try to capture fully the breadth and depth of approaches to thinking and making that charge our studios, classrooms, labs, and shops. While some of this variety is reflected in this collection of essays, any anthology is challenged conceptually not just by who is included but also by how many others with valuable voices are not. At RISD we have extraordinary faculty and staff and it would be impossible to not miss many of those voices. These dedicated individuals transform students while they attend the college, but their contributions also extend far into and throughout the stages of life after RISD. At every alumni event someone always recounts a treasured comment from a memorable critique, expresses gratitude for valued mentorship, or articulates a transformative assignment, the challenge of which continues to guide them.

Parents, too, comment on the creativity, knowledge, and new perspectives they have gained from witnessing their son or daughter grow through his or her education in art and design. Similarly, employers cite the value of the intelligence and expertise as well as the work ethic that result from our teaching and learning practices. Every day, our faculty guide young artists and designers to challenge themselves beyond what they thought they could achieve, to see with an intensity and honesty they didn't know was possible, and to translate a range of skills and concepts into new and personally invented territories. To the faculty, museum curators, librarians, and staff who together have defined this rich, creative learning environment we are grateful. Each step in the path to developing creative thinkers and critical makers who can innovate to shape our world is possible because of the remarkable work you do.

We would also like to thank Richard Narramore, Senior Editor, John Wiley & Sons, Inc., for recognizing the broad potential of art and design education, and for challenging us to articulate how and why as leaders in this domain, we have something unique and timely to share. Working with writers representing such diverse voices and varied approaches has been complex and rewarding. Jennifer Liese, Director of our Writing Center, worked diligently and closely with our distinguished writers to shape, structure, expand, and clarify their essays—engaging them in her own form of critique. Additionally, Thomas Brendler, Tim Murphy, and Kara Mason contributed to editing some of the chapters. A book about art and design has to be visually satisfying and functionally smart, and Julie Fry transformed our ideas into a beautiful object, reflective of its content. With Julie we chose the Dispatch font by RISD Graphic Design alumnus Cyrus Highsmith. Our sincere thanks to each of you for joining us in this venture and elevating the caliber of the final result.

President John Maeda has always believed that what we do at RISD needs to be more visible to a world that needs art and design. We thank him for inspiring us to bring the voices of our faculty and staff to new audiences, and for his steadfast support of our work.

Finally, our families—Paul, Angela, and Lucas, and Isabel and Annise—deserve special thanks. They encouraged us to undertake this challenge on top of our existing professional commitments and surrendered those extra minutes and hours in our busy days, without which this book would have remained a rough sketch. We thank them for always inspiring us to do more, and for their unique gifts, which give meaning to the "critical making" of this book—a book we hope will enrich our readers' experience as we share the transformative qualities of a rigorous art and design education.

—Rosanne Somerson and Mara L. Hermano

Contributors

DANIEL CAVICCHI is Dean of Liberal Arts at Rhode Island School of Design. He is author of *Tramps Like Us: Music and Meaning Among Springsteen Fans* (Oxford University Press, 1998) and *Listening and Longing: Music Lovers in the Age of Barnum* and co-editor of *My Music: Explorations of Music in Daily Life* (Wesleyan University Press, 2011 and 1993). His public work has included *Songs of Conscience, Sounds of Freedom* (2008), an inaugural exhibit for the Grammy Museum in Los Angeles; the curriculum accompanying Martin Scorsese's *The Blues* film series; and other projects with the Public Broadcasting System and the National Park Service. He is currently the editor of *Music/Interview*, a new book series from Wesleyan University Press. In addition to several research grants and awards, Cavicchi is the recipient of both the President's Award for Excellence in Teaching from Brown University and the John R. Frazier Award for Excellence in Teaching from Rhode Island School of Design.

KELLY DOBSON, Assistant Professor and Department Head, Digital + Media, is an artist working in the realms of new media, machine design, social interventions, and public performance. Her projects involve technological systems and the exploration of what they mean and do for people other than the purpose for which they were consciously made. She earned her doctorate at MIT while a member of the Computing Culture Group in the Media Lab and the Interrogative Design Group in MIT's Visual Studies Program. Prior to RISD, she taught at Cornell University and Oslo National Academy of the Arts, and worked as a researcher at MIT's Center for Advanced Visual Studies. Awards include the Rockefeller New Media Artist Fellowship, the Franklin Furnace Fund for Performance Art Award, and the VIDA Art and Artificial Life Honor. Her work has been featured in many publications and exhibited internationally, including at Witte de With in Rotterdam, Circulo De Bellas Artes in Madrid, the Millennium Museum in Beijing, Goldsmiths College in London, Fringe Exhibitions in Los Angeles, and The Kitchen, The Museum of Modern Art, Gigantic Art Space, Eyebeam, and Exit Art in New York City.

JOHN DUNNIGAN, Professor and Department Head, Furniture Design, is a designer, maker, and educator. His work has been shown in more than 100 exhibitions, including ten solo exhibitions, and is in private and public collections including those of the Museum of Fine Arts, Boston, and The Smithsonian American Art Museum in Washington, DC. Dunnigan's furniture has been featured in the *New York Times*, *Newsweek*, and the *Boston Globe* and in books and catalogues such as *New American Furniture*. He is a partner in DEZCO furniture design llc, a company dedicated to sustainable practices in design for mass production. Dunnigan has been a member of the faculty at RISD in the departments of Industrial Design, Interior Architecture, and Furniture Design and previously served as Interim Dean of the Division of Architecture + Design. Building RISD's capacity for interdisciplinary research, he was co-PI of NSF Experimental Program for Competitive Research at RISD from 2009 to 2012.

SARAH GANZ BLYTHE is Director of Education at the Rhode Island School of Design Museum and was previously Director of Interpretation and Research at The Museum of Modern Art, New York. She collaborates with artists and designers to realize exhibitions, commissions, events, and publications for varied audiences. Recent projects explore the conditions and methods of creative practice through the material evidence of historical and contemporary art and design. She is the author of *Looking at Dada* with Edward Powers and editor with John Elderfield of *Modern Painting and Sculpture: 1880 to the Present* (The Museum of Modern Art, 2006 and 2010). Her writing on modern and contemporary art, exhibition culture, pedagogy, and interpretation practices has appeared in numerous scholarly publications and museum catalogues. She is a regular contributor to programs nationally and internationally, including at the Tate and Victoria & Albert Museum, London, and the Banff Center, Canada. Ganz Blythe teaches in Graduate Studies at RISD and at the Center for Public Humanities at Brown University, Providence. She holds a PhD in art history from the Institute of Fine Arts, New York University.

MARA L. HERMANO, Executive Director of Strategic Planning and Academic Initiatives, oversees the implementation of RISD's strategic initiatives and is responsible for institutional accreditation and assessment. Born in Manila, she left to study art history—not from slides—and received her BA from Sarah Lawrence College and MA from the Institute of Fine Arts, New York University. Hermano pursued her interest in cultural intersections, art, and design at New York arts organizations including the auction house Christie's and the Frick Art Reference Library, before discovering the opportunities and challenges of art school administration, first at the Sam Fox School of Design and Visual Arts, Washington University in St. Louis, and then at RISD, where she initially served as Special Assistant to the President. Hermano is the editor of *Spanish Artists from the Fourth to the Twentieth Century: A Critical Dictionary*, vols. 3–4 (GK Hall, 1996) and *Lamesa: The Filipino Table* (Santa Barbara Publishing, 1999), and co-author of *At Home with Filipino Art and Artists* (Anvil Publishing, 2001).

LESLIE HIRST, Associate Professor, Foundation Studies, is a visual artist who has exhibited in the United States and Europe. She holds a BFA from the School of the Art Institute of Chicago and an MFA from the Maryland Institute College of Art. Hirst works in a variety of media to explore the meaning of materiality. Using found objects, she deconstructs the repetitive symbols and messages of everyday experience, then reconfigures, embellishes, and elevates these objects to reflect the complexity of an interconnected world. Her compositions and installations suggest a type of mapping of the human environment, referencing street plans and growth patterns as a means for navigating an inhabited landscape. Hirst comes by these sensibilities instinctively, through her experience as a distance runner, as the elements of time and the traveled path form an indelible connection to the earth and a definition of "place." Recent projects examine the way in which the visible word is woven into the social context of societies. In particular, she explores the role of the materiality of the written word through the semiotics of marks as language. Hirst has received a fellowship from the Rhode Island State Council on the Arts and grants from the North Carolina Arts Council, and has been awarded several artist residencies.

LUCINDA HITCHCOCK, Professor, Graphic Design, teaches in both the graduate and undergraduate programs at RISD. The courses she teaches—"Making Meaning," "Typography," "Type and Message in the Built Environment," and "Visual Narrative," to name a few—reflect her interest in the relationship between language, design, typography, and text. She has a BA in English from Kenyon College, an MA in English Literature from Columbia University, and an MFA in Graphic Design from Yale University. Her research areas include book design, conceptual applications for design and typography, visual and written language in three dimensions, and the creation and critique of visual narrative. Lucinda Hitchcock Design produces books and other printed material for publishers and arts organizations including the Museum of Fine Arts, Boston, and the Metropolitan Museum of Art, New York. Her designs have won several awards and have appeared in AIGA annuals, *Print Magazine*, Best of New England exhibitions, and the American Association of University Presses "best-of-shows" and catalogues. Hitchcock's work, along with selected student work, appeared in *Type Design: Radical Innovations and Experimentation*, edited by Teal Triggs (Thames & Hudson, 2003).

JOHN MAEDA is a leader who imagines how design can simplify technology and help leaders respond to new challenges in the era of social media. His work as a graphic designer, computer scientist, artist, and educator earned him the distinction of being named one of the 75 most influential people of the twenty-first century by *Esquire*. In June 2008, Maeda became president of Rhode Island School of Design, and in late 2012, *Business Insider* named RISD the #1 design school in the world. At RISD, Maeda is leading the movement to transform STEM (Science, Technology, Engineering, and Math) to STEAM by adding Art. Called the "Steve Jobs of academia" by *Forbes*, he believes art and design are poised to transform our economy in the twenty-first century as science and technology did in the last century. Maeda previously served as associate director of research at the MIT Media Lab. He serves on the boards of Sonos, Quirky, and Wieden+Kennedy, and on the Davos World Economic Forum's Global Agenda Council on New Models of Leadership. His books include *The Laws of Simplicity*, *Creative Code*, and *Redesigning Leadership*, which expands on his Twitter feed at @johnmaeda, one of *TIME* magazine's 140 Best Twitter Feeds of 2012. Maeda received the AIGA Medal in 2010 and his work is in the permanent collection of The Museum of Modern Art.

NEAL OVERSTROM is a biologist, designer, educator, and Director of RISD's Nature Lab. His work has focused on promoting environmental literacy through informal learning experiences. Prior to RISD he held senior posts for exhibit development and zoological management at the Mystic Aquarium and was a design associate with Kent+Frost Landscape Architecture. He earned a BS in biology from the University of Connecticut, an MA in zoology from Connecticut College, and a Master of Landscape Architecture from the University of Massachusetts, Amherst. In 2009 he was named the University of Massachusetts Olmsted Scholar, for his work on exploring the intersection of living systems, technology, and aesthetics in designing for sustainability. His current interests involve investigating biological influences on design, particularly the ways in which pattern, form, and living elements in the built environment can reinforce the human-nature connection.

PATRICIA C. PHILLIPS is Dean of Graduate Studies at RISD. Her research and critical writing focus on contemporary public art, architecture, sculpture, and landscape, and the intersection of these areas. She is the author of *Ursula von Rydingsvard: Working* (Prestel, 2011) and *It Is Difficult*, a survey of the work of Alfredo Jaar (Actar Press, 1998). Her curatorial and design projects include *Disney Animators and Animation* (Whitney Museum of Art,

1981), *The POP Project* (Institute for Contemporary Art/P.S. 1, 1988), and *Making Sense: Five Installations on Sensation* (Katonah Museum of Art, 1996). In 1996, she curated *City Speculations*, a major exhibition at the Queens Museum of Art, and edited the accompanying catalogue of the same title (Princeton Architectural Press, 1996). From 2002 to 2007, she served as editor-in-chief of *Art Journal*, a quarterly publication on contemporary art published by the College Art Association. She is on the editorial advisory boards of *Public Art Review*, *Imagining America: Public*, and *Public Art Dialogue*, where she also serves as book review editor.

PRADEEP SHARMA, Dean of Architecture and Design, started life in the sciences and retrained as a product designer. He has extensive international experience in art and design as an educator, researcher, and consultant in product design, design strategy, branding, creativity, and innovation. His current research work is in complex responsive processes leading to creative action. Prior to joining RISD, he was Head of the Bath School of Art and Design at Bath Spa University, Head of Art and Design at the Cardiff School of Creative and Cultural Studies at the University of Glamorgan, and a research fellow and senior lecturer at Unitec Institute of Technology in New Zealand. He holds a BA and MA in Electrical and Information Sciences from Cambridge University, an MA in Industrial Design Engineering from Teesside University, and is completing his Doctorate in Management at the University of Hertfordshire.

ROSANNE SOMERSON is a furniture designer/maker, educator, and Provost and chief academic officer at RISD. She simultaneously maintains a robust creative practice, designing and creating furniture for exhibitions and commissions. Additionally, she consults on innovative educational and creative practice for institutions and industry. Her work has been exhibited widely throughout the world and is represented in many prestigious private, corporate, and museum collections, including the Museum of Fine Arts, Boston, the Renwick Collection of the National Museum of American Art, Washington, DC, the Yale University Art Gallery, the Huntsville Museum of Art, and the RISD Museum. She has served on the boards of the Haystack Mountain School, in Maine, the Society of Arts and Crafts, Boston, is a named Fellow of the American Craft Council, and is the subject of an interview that forms part of the Smithsonian Institute Archives of American Art Oral History Program. As a sought-after international lecturer, juror, exhibitor, and evaluator, she applies both local and global perspectives to her work. She has received numerous awards and citations for her work as a designer, artist, and teacher, most recently the Award of Distinction for lifetime achievement in the field of studio furniture by the Furniture Society.

EVA SUTTON, Professor, Photography, is a digital media artist, photographer, and programmer whose work explores the boundary between static images and interactive databases. Before becoming an artist, Sutton was a software engineer working in biotechnology and large-scale database management. Her work has been exhibited at venues including Aperture Gallery, SF CameraWork, Exit Art (New York), The Tang Museum, The Philadelphia Museum of Art, The National Center of Photography in Paris, Museo Tridentino, Trento, Italy, Trondelag Center for Contemporary Art in Norway, and SIGGRAPH. She has lectured on issues in art and technology at Princeton, New York University, The Cooper Union, The American Museum of Natural History, Hong Kong Center for the Arts, and The Ludwig Foundation in Havana, Cuba. Her work has been featured in *Aperture*, the *New Yorker*, *Harpers*, the *New York Times*, and *Leonardo*. Sutton holds a BA in Architecture from North Carolina State University and an MFA in Computer Art from the School of Visual Arts, New York. Her research and teaching at RISD is focused on the relationship between photography and time-based media. Her current photographic work explores the phenomenon of displacement, in particular squatter communities in marginalized urban environments and diasporic communities.

FRANK R. WILSON was a founder and is a former Medical Director of the Health Program for Performing Artists at the University of California, San Francisco. He was Guest Professor of Neurology at the University of Düsseldorf, Germany, from 1989 to 1990, and Clinical Professor of Neurology, Stanford University School of Medicine, from 2001 until his retirement from clinical practice in 2004. He has written extensively about the neurological basis of human hand skill, and is the author of *The Hand: How Its Use Shapes the Brain, Language, and Human Culture* (Pantheon Books, 1998), which was nominated by the publisher that year for a Pulitzer Prize in nonfiction. Wilson is a 2012 recipient of an Honorary Doctorate in Fine Arts from the Massachusetts College of Art and Design in Boston, and a 2013 recipient of a Goldman Sachs consulting fellowship to The Jerome and Dorothy Lemelson Center for the Study of Invention and Innovation at the Smithsonian Institute in Washington, DC.

Illustrations

1 Laura Kishimoto (BFA 2013 Furniture Design), *Medusa*, 2013, acrylic and aluminum rivets, 5×12×12 in.

2 Daniel Cho (BFA 2015 Industrial Design), *Visual Illusion*, 2012, found objects and spotlight, installation view and inspiration (poster image: Robert Doisneau, *Musician in the Rain*, 1957)

3 Anthony Dahut (BFA 2015 Furniture Design), *First Person, Singular* (installation view and detail), 2012, video projection and brush PHOTO OF BRUSH: ERIK GOULD

4 Anna Riley (BFA 2014 Glass), *Set in the City* (details), 2010, wood, Plexiglas, graph paper, ink, mechanized arm, and spotlight, dimensions variable (12 platforms, each 12×12 in.)

5 Eun Sang (Ernie) Lee (BFA 2015 Furniture Design), *Color Play*, 2008, gouache on paper mounted to book board covered with book cloth

6 Eun Sang (Ernie) Lee, *Untitled*, 2011

7 Adam Gault and Stefanie Augustine (BFA 1999 Film/Animation/Video and BFA 1999 Illustration), *The Gettysburg Address* (stills), 2010, black-and-white animation, 3:05 minutes

8 Seth Snyder (BFA 2008 Industrial Design) on a "blind walk," Providence, 2008

9 Margaret Kearney (BFA 2013 Textiles), *Weaving Detroit*, 2012, wool, cotton, rayon, metallic thread, 72×54 in.

10 Michael Mergen (MFA 2011 Photography), *Jury Room 706, Tulsa, OK*, 2010, from the series "Deliberate," archival pigment print, 16×16 in.

11 Michael Mergen, *Ceremony, Room #1, New York, NY*, 2011, from the series "Naturalization," archival pigment print, 16×16 in.

12 Brittany Bennett (BFA 2011 Textiles), *Doll*, 2009, pecan, muslin, and wool, 16×2×4 in.

13 Rebecca Manson (BFA 2011 Ceramics), *Polyrhythmic Stool*, 2009, pecan, 20×12×14 in.

14 Felicia Hung (BFA 2013 Furniture Design), *Treaty of Portsmouth*, 2010, cherry and silver maple, 18×36×60 in.

15 Drawing exercise in the Painting department

16 Drawing exercise in the Industrial Design department

17 Christine Zavesky (BArch 2008), *Bridge Study*, 2008, graphite and linseed oil on paper, 60×45 in.

18   Daedalus presenting the cow to Pasiphae, Roman fresco in the House of the Vetti, Pompeii, first century CE. Gianni Dagli Orti/The Art Archive at Art Resource, NY

19   Matthias Pleissnig (BFA 2003 Furniture Design), *Providence*, 2008, steam-bent white oak, 132×80×36 in.

20   Rich Brilliant Willing (Theo Richardson, Charles Brill, and Alex Williams, all BFA 2006 Furniture Design), *Bias Clock*, 2010, 12¼×3¼ in.

21   Rich Brilliant Willing, *Bright Side of Life*, 2010, cast glass, 8⁹/₁₀×4⁴/₅ in.

22   Jamie Wolfond (BFA 2013 Furniture Design), *Frumpy Chairs*, 2012, low-density polyethylene plastic, approx. 17³/₄×21³/₄×29¹/₂ in.

23   Daniel Michalik (MFA 2004 Furniture Design), *Cortiça Chaise Longue*, 2006, 100% recycled cork, 26×20×74 in.   PHOTO: JASON MADARA

24   Tanya Aguiñiga (MFA 2005 Furniture Design), *Hole Table*, 2005, powder-coated steel, 29×40 in.

25   Sarah Pease (BFA 2013 Furniture Design), sketchbook, 2013   PHOTO: ERIK GOULD

26   Timothy Liles (BFA 2005 Furniture Design), *Be Well Chair*, 2005, maple, sanitary crepe paper, aluminum, 36×16×17 in.

27   Charles Eames (American, 1907–1978) and Ray Eames (American, 1912–1988), designers; Evans Products Co. (American, 1946–1949), manufacturer, *Leg Splint for U.S. Navy*, ca. 1943, molded plywood, 42 in. (length)   GIFT OF DR. AND MRS. ARMAND VERSACI, MUSEUM OF ART RHODE ISLAND SCHOOL OF DESIGN, PROVIDENCE

28   Providence Painter (Name Vase), Greek, Storage jar (amphora) with Apollo with lyre, ca. 500–475 BCE, terracotta, red-figure, 20 in. (height)   GIFT OF MRS. GUSTAV RADEKE, MUSEUM OF ART RHODE ISLAND SCHOOL OF DESIGN, PROVIDENCE

29   Egyptian, from Abydos, excavated in 1895, furniture support in the form of a bull's leg, ca. 2800 BCE, hippopotamus ivory, 4⁷/₈ in. (height)   HELEN M. DANFORTH ACQUISITION FUND, MUSEUM OF ART RHODE ISLAND SCHOOL OF DESIGN, PROVIDENCE

30   Japanese, Noh theater costume (*karaori*), eighteenth century, ikat-dyed silk, compound weave with supplementary continuous gold-leaf paper patterning wefts and supplementary discontinuous silk patterning weft floats, 57 in. (center back length)   GIFT OF MISS LUCY T. ALDRICH, MUSEUM OF ART RHODE ISLAND SCHOOL OF DESIGN, PROVIDENCE

31   Claude Monet (French, 1840–1926), *The Basin at Argenteuil*, 1874, oil on canvas, 21³/₄×29¹/₄ in.   GIFT OF MRS. MURRAY S. DANFORTH, MUSEUM OF ART RHODE ISLAND SCHOOL OF DESIGN, PROVIDENCE

32   Installation view of *Painting Air: Spencer Finch*, 2012, Museum of Art Rhode Island School of Design, Providence   PHOTO: ERIK GOULD

33   Angela Bulloch (Canadian, b. 1966), *Copper 2*, 2011, two copper pixel boxes with DMX control unit, each pixel box 19⁷/₈ × 19⁷/₈ × 19⁷/₈ in.   RICHARD BROWN BAKER FUND FOR CONTEMPORARY BRITISH ART, MUSEUM OF ART RHODE ISLAND SCHOOL OF DESIGN, PROVIDENCE

34   Agustina Bello Decurnex (MFA 2013 Textiles), *Tidal*, 2012, silk, thermoplastic poly, dyes

35   Anjali Srinivasan (MFA 2007 Glass), *999 Fragments of Puffy Glass*, 2007, glass and flour, 3 × 3 × 9 ft.   PHOTO: MIN JEONG SONG

36   Jacob von Falke, *Art in the House* (Boston: L. Prang and Company, 1878)

37   Diana Wagner (Master of Industrial Design 2014), *Oh Snap, Material Transformation + Attachments*, 2012, recycled high density polyethylene (HDPE), recycled polyethylene terephthalate (PET), felt, fabric, paper, aluminum, and hardware, 21 samples, each 1³/₄ × 1³/₄ in.

38   Emmi Laakso and Robin Davis (both BFA 2011 Graphic Design), *Sink or Swim*, 2011, Styrofoam and paint, dimensions variable

39   Jerel Johnson (MFA 2014 Graphic Design), *Grotesque*, digital poster, dimensions variable

40   Kai Salmela (BFA 2006 Graphic Design), *Market House Hatchmarks*, 2006, digital projection

41   Lauren Sun (BFA 2009 Graphic Design), "Type History" project, 2007, inkjet prints, 16 × 16 in.

42   Aaron Shoon (MFA 2006 Graphic Design), "Type 2" book project, 2005, hand-bound book, paper, cloth, board, approx. 6 × 9 in.

43   Wasily Davidov (BFA 2005 Graphic Design), *OUCH*, 2005, installation views, letters made of poster board, foam core, glue, each letter approx. 36 × 40 in.

44   Rebecca Zhang (BFA 2015 Graphic Design), pictograms, 2012, inkjet, toner on paper, approx. 5 × 5 in.

45   Jessica Greenfield (MFA 2011 Graphic Design), *Lessons Learned from the Physical World*, 2010, inkjet print, approx. 20 × 26 in.

46   Micah Barrett (BFA 2012 Graphic Design), *Feeding America*, 2009, inkjet print, approx. 24 × 36 in.

47 Wael Morcos (MFA 2013 Graphic Design), *Einstein's Dreams*, 2012, inkjet on newsprint, 15 1/2 × 12 in.

48 MFA Graphic Design Class of 2011, *This Is the Catalog of the Show*, 2011, ink, newsprint, approx. 30 × 22 in. open

49 Edna Lawrence Nature Lab PHOTO: DAVID O'CONNOR

50 Edna W. Lawrence, 1951 PHOTO: ED HOWELL (BFA 1951 ILLUSTRATION); ARCHIVES OF THE FLEET LIBRARY AT RHODE ISLAND SCHOOL OF DESIGN

51 Edna Lawrence, compositions of seashells on linen in typewriter ribbon boxes, 1952–1954, each 3 in. diameter PHOTO: ERIK GOULD

52 Olivia Verdugo (MFA 2011 Graphic Design), *Quiet Storms*, 2011, digital media from watercolor based on microscope images (foreground image: Kim Krans, *The Wild Unknown*, www.thewildunknown.com)

53 Zoe Wendel (BFA 2011 Jewelry + Metalsmithing), *Rabbit Skeleton Necklace*, 2010, laser cut brass, 12 × 8 in.

54 Zoe Wendel, *Spider Web Necklace*, 2010, silver chain, 17 × 7 in.

55 James H. Mathewson, diagram of "master images" of science, from "The Visual Core of Science: Definitions and Applications to Education," *International Journal of Science Education* 27 (2005): 529–548

56 Christina Kazakia (Master of Industrial Design 2011), *Stick-Lets*, 2011

57 Christina Bertoni, critique diagram, 2013

58 Elliott Romano (BFA 2013 Photography), critique diagram, 2013

59 Norm Paris, critique diagram, 2013

60 Ian Stell (MFA 2012 Furniture Design), critique diagram, 2013

61 Daniel Hewett, critique diagram, 2013 PHOTO: ERIK GOULD

62 Eva Sutton, critique diagram, 2013

63 "Design for Extreme Environments: Common Crew Cabin," with NASA, 2011 PHOTO: ANSON CHEUNG

64 "The Green Studio," with Kimberly-Clark, 2010 PHOTO: BETH MOSHER

65 "Makers Gonna Make," Tattly temporary tattoo, designed by Jude Landry PHOTO: CARLY AYRES AND SARAH PEASE

Index

A

Abductive reasoning, 238–239
Acosta, Silvia, 74, 77, 80, 83, 84, 92
Action:
    identity and, 15–16
    joint, 240–241
    materials as agents of, 139, 146–147,
    149–150, 161, 163
Agamben, Giorgio, 123
Aguiñiga, Tanya, 108, 110–111
Albers, Josef, 48
Anderson, Eric, 138, 151–156
Application, as rule-based standard, 39
Architecture, 56, 79, 80, 84
Ariely, Dan, 239
Art:
    breaking rules in, 39–40
    critical role of, 9
    digital, 5, 6
    as rule-based, 37–39
Art and design education. *See also*
    Critical making; *specific topics*
    art and design school learning
    model, 19
    emulation in, 117–118
    essential components of, 35
    intentions of, 29
    recent surge of interest in, 27–28
    in STEAM model, 8, 28
    thingking in, 98
Art in the House (Jacob von Falke), 152, 153
Artists and designers:
    as change agents, 9
    delineations between, 29
    as form givers, 95
    as hosts for creative discovery, 28
    knowledge required for, 40
    as laborers, 37
    makers vs., 33
Auerbach, Tauba, 37
Augustine, Stefanie, 57–59
Ayres, Carly, 247

B

Ball Ottomans (Jamie Wolfond), 105
Barrett, Micah, 183–185
Barthes, Roland, 55
The Basin at Argenteuil (Claude Monet), 128, 129
Becker, Carol, 135
Becker, Howard, 55
Beckett, Samuel, 40
Bello Decurnex, Agustina, 144, 145
Bennett, Brittany, 64, 65
Benyus, Janine, 200
Bertoni, Christina, 210, 213–215, 217, 218, 221–224, 227
Be Well Chair (Timothy Liles), 113–115
Bias Clock (Rich Brilliant Willing), 102, 103
Biomechanics, 11–14
Biomimicry, 200
Biophilia, 204–205
Blackburn, Jean, 123
"Blind walk" (Seth Snyder), 57, 59
Books, 151–154, 173
Brain, 13, 14, 97
Bridge Study (Christine Zavesky), 84, 85
Bright Side of Life (Rich Brilliant Willing), 102, 103
Brill, Charles, 100, 102, 103
Bringhurst, Robert, 174
Broholm, Dale, 61
Bulloch, Angela, 132, 133
Business. *See also* Partnered engagements
    creativity's importance in, 8
    design in, 28, 231

C

Castle, James, 87
Cavicchi, Daniel, 22–23, 52–72, 247, 255
Ceremony Room #1, New York, NY
    (Michael Mergen), 62, 63
Chihuly, Dale, 6
Cho, Daniel, 41–43
Close, Chuck, 40

Collage, 86, 196, 198

Color Play (Eun Sang [Ernie] Lee), 48

Computer-aided design and fabrication, 7

Computers, 16–17n.4. *See also* Technologies

Context, 53, 171–172

Contextual thinking, 22–23, 52–72

    and academic work, 70–71

    in creating studio objects, 68–69

    and cultural expression, 43

    defined, 53

    examples of, 57–61

    and overvaluation of textuality, 54–55

    relationship of textual thinking and, 55–56

    in RISD program, 55–57, 71

    textual thinking vs., 53

    transformative nature of, 71–72

    in Witness Tree Project, 61, 63–69

Copper 2 (Angela Bulloch), 132, 133

Corn Stories (Margaret Kearney), 61

Cortiça Chaise Longue (Daniel Michalik),
    107–109

The Creation of Adam (Michelangelo), 15

Creative problem solving, 39, 40

Creative process, 37, 211. *See also* Thingking

    object lessons in, 120, 121

    physical skill supporting/enlivening, 15–16

    trust in uncertainty of, 35

Creativity, 242

    in art and design school learning model, 19

    as behavior, 231, 232

    in business, 8, 28

    nature and nurture in, 34

    originality vs., 38–39

    psychological and behavioral
    view of, 34

    RISD alumni's applications of, 20–21

    social context of, 55

    teaching, 34

    from tension between rules
    and imagination, 38

Critical making, 19–31, 98

    applications of, 20–21

    contexts informing the maker in, 22–23

    critical thinking and making merged in, 24

    critiques in, 26–27

    defined, 32

    and drawing, 23–24, 87

    first-year experience in, 22.
    See also Groundwork

    learning from nature's systems in, 26

    learning from objects in, 24–25

    making meaning in, 25–26

    materials in, 25

    partnered engagements in, 27

    and physicality of human perception/
    thought/action, 14

    at RISD, 7–8, 245, 247–249

    thinking and making merged in,
    see Thingking

Critical thinking, 24, 98, 132

Critiques ("crits"), 210–229

    concurrence of threads in, 220–222

    connections made in, 215, 227

    dealing with challenges in, 217

    defined, 211

    description vs. judgment in, 213–214, 217

    effective models of, 221

    formation of ideas in, 226, 228

    institutional, 131–133

    limitations of language in, 228–229

    as mazes, 222–223

    in Partnered Studios, 232, 235

    scenarios occurring during, 218–219

    scope of conversation in, 223–225, 227

    of students' works, 26–27, 95

    visual representations of, 211–213, 216,
    219, 220, 225, 226

D

Dahut, Anthony, 43–45

Davidov, Wasily, 178, 179

Davis, Robin, 167, 168

Design:

    breaking rules in, 39–40

critical role of, 9
digital, 5, 6
process in, 236–238
as rule-based, 37–39
Design by Numbers system, 6
Designers, *see* Artists and designers
The Detection Table (Timothy Liles), 113
Dewey, John, 68–69, 126, 241
Digital art and design, 5, 6
Dion, Mark, 196
Discovery, 37, 88, 104
Dobson, Kelly, 25, 138–163, 247, 256
Doll (Brittany Bennett), 64, 65
Dorner, Alexander, 135
Drawing, 74–93
    codependency of, 83
    in contemporary art, 76–77
    and critical making, 23–24, 87
    differing definitions of, 83–84, 86
    digital approaches to, 86
    "expanded field" of, 75
    functional, 81
    goal of, 88
    historical trajectory of, 76, 77
    as ideation, 81
    learning of, 77, 79
    physical nature of, 80
    students' relationships to, 79, 80
    teaching of, 79–81, 88–93
    and writing, 111
Drawing Center (New York), 75
Duchamp, Marcel, 55
Dunnigan, John, 24, 94–115, 155, 256
Dutton, Denis, 205
Dwiggins, William Addison, 165–166

E

Eames, Charles and Ray, 120, 121
Edna Lawrence Nature Lab, 8, 26, 115n.3, 167,
    190–207, 247
    biological guides to design in, 198–201
    hands-on learning at, 191–195

and the human-nature connection,
    204–207
microscopes and micro-imaging systems
    at, 202–204
organization of, 195–198
Education. *See also* Art and design education
    change in, 248
    grades and assessment in, 39–40
    influence of technologies/media on,
    16–17n.4
    RISD's model for, 19–20. *See also*
    Critical making
    STEM and STEAM in, 7, 8, 28
Einstein's Dreams (Wael Morcos), 186, 187
Embodied knowledge, 97, 98
Entrepreneurship, 9, 231, 232
Evolution, 11–14, 16n.1
Exploration, 75, 89

F

Failure, 90, 104, 241–242
Feeding America (Micah Barrett), 183–185
Fellowships, 232, 235–236
Fiber, 140–145
Finch, Spencer, 128–131
First Person, Singular (Anthony Dahut),
    43–45
Fisher, Jean, 75, 93n.
Fleet Library, 24–25, 115n.3, 156
Foucault, Michel, 240
Foundation Studies, *see* Groundwork
Frazer, Colin, 186, 187
Frazier, John R., 56
Frensch, Peter, 39
Frumpy Chairs (Jamie Wolfond), 105–107
Fry, Ben, 6
Fuller, Buckminster, 238–239
Furniture design, 98–113, 120, 155

G

Ganz Blythe, Sarah, 24, 116–136, 255
Gault, Adam, 57–59

The Gettysburg Address (Adam Gault and Stefanie Augustine), 57–59

Ginzel, Andrew, 51n.5

Glantzman, Judith, 118–119

Glass, 144, 146–150

Gould, Glenn, 55

Gould, Stephen Jay, 191

Graham Visual + Material Resource Center (MRC), 25, 156–161

Graphic design, 134–135, 165–189

    context in, 56

    goals of, 167, 171

    graduate studies in, 186–189

    meaning making in, 181, 183–186

    role of graphic designers, 165–166

    storytelling in, 171–174

    typography in, 174–179

    visual linguistics in, 178, 180–182

Greenfield, Jessica, 181–183

Grotesque (Jerel Johnson), 167, 169

Groundwork, 32–50

    as breaking down to build back up, 36–37

    discovery in, 37

    for finding authentic voice and direction, 34–35

    importance of creative process over product in, 37

    inviting possibilities in, 35

    rule breaking in, 39–40

    rules-based standards in, 37–39

    students' role in, 35–36

    taking all steps toward goals in, 46, 48

    testing options in, 40–41

    using sketchbooks in, 45–46

    vision/visibility in, 41, 43, 45

H

Habermas, Jürgen, 135

Halley, Peter, 83

Hand, 11–14, 16n.1, 97

Harkett, Daniel, 125

Hermano, Mara L., 245–249, 257

Hewett, Daniel, 210, 214, 215, 217, 221–225, 228

Hirst, Leslie, 22, 32–50, 257–258

Hitchcock, Lucinda, 25–26, 164–189, 258

Hole Table (Tanya Aguiñiga), 108, 110–111

Holman, Cas, 74, 77, 80–81, 84, 86–92

Hoptman, Laura, 93n.

Horii, Ken, 88–89

Hughes, Holly, 120

Humans:

    hand and wrist evolution in, 11–14

    human-nature connection, 204–207

    innate giftedness of, 11

    reciprocity between action and identity in, 15–16

Hung, Felicia, 64, 67

I

Industrial design, 56, 57, 80–81, 86, 91, 103

Innovation, 242–243

    in business, 28

    curricular models encouraging, 20

    as process, 231–232

Innovation Studios, 232, 235

Integrated learning, 29, 111–113

Intelligence, 15, 97, 140

Interpretation, 41, 43, 45, 125–126, 128

J

Jakobson, Roman, 69

Johanson, Donald, 11

Johnson, Jerel, 167, 169

Johnson, Lee, 120, 122–123

Jury Room 706, Tulsa, OK (Michael Mergen), 62, 63

K

Kazakia, Christina, 206, 207

Kearney, Margaret, 59–61

Keil, Charles, 70

Kellert, Stephen, 207

Kernaghan, Brian, 131–132

Kishomoto, Laura, 30, 31
Knowledge, 40, 96–98
Krauss, Rosalind, 93
Kripke, Elizabeth, 247, 249

L
Laakso, Emmi, 167, 168
Landry, Jude, 246, 247
Langevin, James, 8, 28
Language of art and design, 68–69
    and critiques, 214
    deriving meaning of, 125, 174
    forming, 24
    in graphic design, 165, 171
    translating spoken language into, 228
    typography, 174
    verbalizing, 153–154
    visual linguistics, 178, 180–182
    vocabulary of materials, 146–147, 149–150
Lasch, Carol, 119
Lawrence, Edna, 190, 191, 193, 194, 196–198
Learning, 88
    of drawing, 77, 79
    embracing wholeness of, 35
    exploration in, 89
    hands-on, 191–195
    integrated, 29, 111–113
    from nature's systems, 26. See also
    Edna Lawrence Nature Lab
    from objects, 24–25. See also
    Object lessons
    teaching vs., 48, 50, 224, 227
Lee, Eun Sang (Ernie), 48, 49
Lefcourt, Daniel, 74, 77, 80, 81, 84, 86–89,
    91, 93
Leibniz, Gottfried, 139, 162
Lessons Learned from the Physical World
    (Jessica Greenfield), 181–183
Lewin, Kurt, 239
Li, Mengzhuo (Jenny), 202–204
Liberal Arts courses, 23, 56–57, 247.
    See also Contextual thinking

Liles, Timothy, 111, 113–115
Lithographs, 84
Louv, Richard, 205, 207
Lucy (Australopithecus afaransis),
    11–13, 15, 16n.1, 16n.2

M
Maeda, John, 5–9, 28, 248, 258–259
Maharam, Michael, 9
Maharam STEAM Fellows in Applied Art
    and Design, 9
Makers, 33, 36–37, 249
Making. See also Critical making
    communities supporting, 55
    contexts informing, 22–23
    craft vs., 87
    critical importance of, 28
    ethics of, 93
    ideas emerging from, 143–144
    meaning making, 25–26, 181, 183–186
    merging of thinking and, 24.
    See also Thingking
    process of, 6–7, 211
Manson, Rebecca, 64, 66
Market House Hatchmarks (Kai Salmela),
    167, 170, 171
Markzke, Mary, 16n.1
Materials, 138–163
    as agents of action, 139, 146–147, 149–150,
    161, 163
    archive, 156–161
    artifacts, 154–156
    critical importance of, 28
    in critical making, 25
    fiber and textiles, 140–145
    as force and energy, 140, 161
    glass, 144, 146–150
    Graham Visual + Material Resource
    Center, 156–161
    texts and books, 151–154
Materials research, 107–111
Mathewson, James, 203, 204

Meaning:
  critical importance of, 28
  from historical objects, 125–126
  making, 25–26, 181, 183–186
  in relation to materials, 140
  transformed by images, 155–156
The Medication Cabinet (Timothy Liles), 113
Medusa (Laura Kishimoto), 30, 31
Mergen, Michael, 61–63
Michalik, Daniel, 107–109
Michelangelo, 15
Microscopy and micro-imaging, 202–204
Middleton, Margaret, 195
Mishkin, Naomi, 245, 248–249
Missakian, Anais, 126, 138, 140–144
Monet, Claude, 128, 129
Morcos, Wael, 186, 187
Museum objects, learning from,
  see Object lessons
Music, 43, 53, 55, 69–70
Myer, Lane, 237, 241–242

N
Narrative, 178
Nature Lab, *see* Edna Lawrence Nature Lab
Nauman, Bruce, 132
Negahban, Arman, 126–127
999 Fragments of Puffy Glass
  (Anjali Srinivasan), 148, 149

O
Object lessons, 116–136
  in art education, 117
  assigning language to form in, 125–126
  co-curricular opportunities for,
  132, 134–135
  in design education, 117–118
  engaging with objects in, 118–120
  for insight into process/context, 120, 121
  for insights into subject matter,
  120, 122–124
  as "institutional critique," 131–133

  in museums of the future, 135–136
  in negotiating artistic influence, 128–131
  in Textiles program, 126–127
*Oh Snap: Material Transformation +
  Attachments*, 158, 159
Originality:
  creativity vs., 38–39
  curricular models encouraging, 20
OUCH (Wasily Davidov), 178, 179
Overstrom, Neal, 26, 190–207, 259

P
Painting, 56, 83, 97, 118–120, 241
Painting Air: Spencer Finch, 128, 130
Paris, Norm, 210, 214, 217–219, 221, 223, 228
Partnered engagements, 230–243
  in critical making, 27
  key forms of, 232–236
  lessons learned from, 236–242
Partnered Studios, 232–235
Pease, Sarah, 111–113, 247
Peirce, Charles Sanders, 238
Phillips, Patricia C., 23, 74–77, 79, 83, 87–92,
  259–260
Photography, 83, 183
Pictograms, 180
Pleissnig, Matthias, 99–101, 103
Polyrhythmic Stool (Rebecca Manson), 64, 66
Pompelia, Mark, 138, 156–161
Poor, Nicole, 185–186
Postman, Neil, 90
Prigogine, Ilya, 240
Prince, Jocelyne, 138, 144–150
Printmaking, 79, 86–87, 119
Process. *See also* Creative process
  in design, 236–238
  of drawing, 75
  innovation as, 231–232
  of making, 6–7, 211
Processing (design system), 6
Providence (Matthias Pleissnig), 100, 101
Prown, Jules, 123

Q

Quiet Storms (Olivia Verdugo), 198, 199

Quilt for a New Community (Margaret Kearney), 59, 61

R

Rabbit Skeleton Necklace (Zoe Wendel), 200, 201

Raftery, Andrew, 74, 76–77, 79, 81, 84, 86–87, 90, 91, 119

Raid the Icebox I (Andy Warhol), 131

Rational-choice theory, 239–240

Reas, Casey, 6

Relational design, 185

Research, 103–104, 107–111

Rhode Island Centennial Committee, 28–29

Rhode Island School of Design (RISD), 6

    alumni of, 20–21, 99, 249

    creation and purpose of, 28–29

    creative learning model of, 19–20.
    See also Critical making

    diverse range of projects at, 19

    first-year experience at, 22.
    See also Groundwork

    goals of students at, 9

    integrity of the work at, 6–7

    Maharam STEAM Fellows in Applied Art and Design, 9

    mission of, 29, 248

    STEAM at, 8

Richardson, Theo, 100, 102, 103

Rich Brilliant Willing (RBW), 100, 102, 103

Riley, Anna, 45–47

RISD Museum, 24, 115n.3, 247

Romano, Elliott, 210, 215–217, 223, 227

Rose, Christopher, 120, 198

Russolo, Luigi, 55

S

Salmela, Kai, 167, 170, 171

Salons, 232, 235

Santacatterini, Stella, 75, 93n.

Schor, Mira, 92

Seeger, Charles, 53, 69

Serra, Richard, 76

Set in the City (Anna Riley), 45–47

Sharma, Pradeep, 27, 230–243, 260

Shoon, Aaron, 175–177

Simpson, Juliette, 195

Sink or Swim (Emmi Laakso and Robin Davis), 167, 168

Sketchbooks, 45–46

Sketching, 80–81, 84, 91

Slager, Henk, 88

Snyder, Seth, 57, 59

Somerson, Rosanne, 7, 19–31, 260–261

Speth, Gus, 207

Spider Web Necklace (Zoe Wendel), 200, 201

Squibb, Eliza, 202–204

Srinivasan, Anjali, 148, 149

STEAM (Science, Technology, Engineering, Arts, and Math), 8, 9, 28

Stell, Ian, 210, 220–224

STEM (Science, Technology, Engineering, and Math), 7, 8, 28

Sternberg, Robert, 39

Stick-Lets (Christina Kazakia), 206, 207

Storr, Robert, 120

Storytelling, 171–174

Subject matter, insights into, 120, 122–124

Sun, Lauren, 175–177

Sutton, Eva, 26–27, 210–229, 261

T

Teaching. *See also individual topics, e.g.:* Drawing

    chance and discovery in prompts/processes, 88–89

    learning vs., 48, 50, 224, 227

    trust between students and teachers, 91

    using obstruction in, 89–90

Technologies:

    and body as agent of mind, 15–16

cost of accepting, 14–15
for digital art and design, 5–6
and drawing, 86
education influenced by, 16–17n.4
for furniture making, 98–99
glass, 147
obsolete, 90
Tepper, Steven J., 248
Text(s):
as materials, 151–154
as term, 53
Textiles, 126–127, 140–145
Textual thinking, 53–56
Thingking, 94–115
ancient underpinnings of, 95–97
in art and design education, 98
defined, 95
in Furniture Design, 98–113
in integrated learning, 111–113
materials research in, 107–111
research in, 103–104
Thinking:
contextual, *see* Contextual thinking
critical, 24, 98, 132
merging of making and, 24.
See also Thingking
talking out loud as, 214
textual, 53–56
This Is the Catalog of the Show, 187–189
Toynbee, Jason, 55
Treaty of Portsmouth (Felicia Hung), 64, 67
Typography, 174–179

U
Ulrich, Roger, 205
Uncertainty, 35, 239–240
Unititled (Eun Sang [Ernie] Lee), 48

V
Van Dijk, Hans, 134
Van Sant, Gus, 6
Verdugo, Olivia, 198, 199
Vision, 41, 43, 45
Visual communication design, 166
Visual Illusion (Daniel Cho), 41–42
Visual linguistics, 178, 180–182
Voice, finding, 34–35, 92
Von Falke, Jacob, 152, 153

W
Wagner, Diana, 158, 159
Warhol, Andy, 55, 131
Waters, Muddy, 43
Weaving Detroit (Margaret Kearney), 60, 61
Weingartner, Charles, 90
The Wellness Project (Timothy Liles), 111, 113
Wendel, Zoe, 200, 201
Williams, Alex, 100, 102, 103
Wilson, E. O., 204–205
Wilson, Frank, 22, 97, 262
Witness Tree Project, 61, 63–69
Wolfond, Jamie, 104–107
Workshops, 232, 235
World Wide Web Wilderness (Colin Frazer), 186

Z
Zavesky, Christine, 84, 85
Zhang, Rebecca, 180
Zimmerman, Henry, 68
Zucker, Kevin, 74, 76, 77, 79, 83, 86, 88–90, 92